Navigating the Business Loan

Guidelines for Financiers, Small-Business Owners, and Entrepreneurs

Navigating the Business Loan
Guidelines for Financiers, Small-Business Owners, and Entrepreneurs

Morton Glantz

AMSTERDAM • BOSTON • HEIDELBERG • LONDON
NEW YORK • OXFORD • PARIS • SAN DIEGO
SAN FRANCISCO • SINGAPORE • SYDNEY • TOKYO

Academic Press is an imprint of Elsevier

Academic Press is an imprint of Elsevier
32 Jamestown Road, London NW1 7BY, UK
525 B Street, Suite 1800, San Diego, CA 92101-4495, USA
225 Wyman Street, Waltham, MA 02451, USA
The Boulevard, Langford Lane, Kidlington, Oxford OX5 1GB, UK

ISBN: 978-0-12-801698-5

British Library Cataloguing-in-Publication Data
A catalogue record for this book is available from the British Library

Library of Congress Cataloging-in-Publication Data
A catalog record for this book is available from the Library of Congress

For information on all Academic Press publications
visit our website at http://store.elsevier.com/

To my wife Maryann
The inspiration, beauty, and love of my life

TABLE OF CONTENTS

FOREWORD

When my best friend, Mort Glantz, asked me to write a foreword for his ninth book, I was both flabbergasted and intimidated. How could I adequately introduce a man recognized as one of the foremost global experts on financial risk management? Mort told me not to worry, and simply asked me to share my story about how I became an entrepreneur, my relationship with risk, and my experience with bankers and investors – a kind of case study, if you will.

I am often asked, "Why are entrepreneurs more tolerant to risk and how did you become an entrepreneur?" My answer is that the notion that entrepreneurs are big risk takers is fundamentally wrong. As an entrepreneur, my relationship with risk is simple. My view is that the best way to make risk more acceptable is to have more direct control over it. In fact, the entrepreneur's two most important skills are the ability to minimize the risk associated with making his or her dreams come true and the ability to run an up-and-coming business. Entrepreneurs are not bigger risk takers than others; we simply have a greater appetite to take accountability for that risk, and spend our energy and focus in managing risk by having more control over it. As an entrepreneur, my biggest fear is being in a situation in which I have little personal control over managing my risk.

My attitude toward risk also explains how I became an entrepreneur. In 1989, I was recently married, I had been in a new job for only 1 year, and I had recently used my vacation days to honeymoon. One evening, my wife and I were watching the news, witnessing the imminent downfall of the Berlin Wall. We locked eyes and said, "Let's go to Berlin and help tear it down!" The next day, I requested a week of unpaid leave, but my boss and HR denied my request. Our division's HR director lectured me about professional priorities, and gave me a choice: my job or Berlin.

I chose Berlin. It was at this moment that I realized that I could not accept a life in which the risks to my well-being, my employment, and my destiny rested in the hands of another person, outside of my control.

I realized that whatever risk was going to be introduced in my life, I would be more likely to accept it if I had a direct and meaningful role in managing it.

So Genny and I flew to Berlin and chipped away at that ominous wall. One week later, with no job to go back to, I decided to start my first business: importing vodka. My goal was to introduce a premium Russian vodka to compete with Stolichnaya, the only Russian vodka sold in the United States. Nine months later, I secured an export license and shipped six containers of my designer Russian vodka to the United States.

Throughout my entrepreneurial career, I learned a great deal about raising growth capital, dealing with bankers, and establishing critical relationships with the right venture capitalists. During those years, I was fortunate to enjoy a close relationship with Morton Glantz, who helped me develop the financials of my last venture's business plan, and who was always available to me for sound business and financial advice.

The first time I needed money to start a business, I was in my early twenties. I was going to take the US vodka market by storm by introducing the first designer vodka from Russia that would be an alternative to Stolichnaya. So, I visited my local bank, where I had banked for many years, and I asked for a $100,000 business loan to launch my venture. Morton had cautioned me that commercial banks do not normally give unsecured loans to new businesses, but are pleased to offer suggestions and advice about alternative choices, such as SBA loans, for example. However, as I attempted to describe my business, the banker kept interrupting with only three words during the meeting: collateral and guarantees. Of course, if I had the funds to provide a guarantee, I would not have needed a loan! Evidently (as Morton cautioned me earlier), as a startup, my company was an unacceptable risk to a commercial bank.

A few days after my disappointing experience with the bank, I had lunch with Morton. I shared my disappointment. Mort laughed and said, "Ara, entrepreneurs don't go to banks to raise startup money. But when you attain growth status, yes – possibly." There was a small caveat, he went on: "Arrive very prepared with a track record supported by a respectable client base, know the rules of the bank lending game, and be ready to inquire about alternative funding sources like **SBA** loans if unsecured or secured loans are not in the cards quite yet."

Thanks to Morton, I learned to be prepared for the variety of questions commercial bankers ask, and was sure to respond with solid facts and figures. I realized that when you approach a lender, you are selling yourself and your confidence in your business plan, as well as your ability to make good on your loan. I was sure to communicate clearly how much money I needed, what I intended to use it for, and exactly how the business loan would be allocated. Frankly, the first banker I met with was probably not insightful enough to assess whether my business was an acceptable risk or not – nor did he really care. I talked to the wrong banker and decided to walk out, never to speak to that bank again.

Morton helped me with a few introductions, and started my quest for the right financial partner, an investor who would share my vision and who would believe it would work. Looking back now at 20 years' worth of entrepreneurial endeavors and the interdependence I shared with my investors, I can see that I made some good decisions, and some bad ones. The following anecdotes will hopefully be useful to you.

- My biggest and most frequent mistake: consistently overestimating revenue projection while underestimating the runway needed and the costs associated with building growth. Consequently, I have spent too much time raising new funds and giving away equity.
- I always overestimated how helpful my bankers would be. Alas, unless you are building a business with concrete assets that can be collateralized by a bank, commercial bankers tend to shy away from entrepreneurs. If you run a software firm, your riches walk in and out of the door every day. Your assets are your people and their ideas – intangibles bankers do not normally accept as collateral.
- If you need growth money but cannot afford to give away any more equity, you may have a hidden asset you can leverage: your client list. At a time when my business was in dire need of growth capital, Mort advised me to consider leveraging my blue-chip client list and the stellar historical payment history I enjoyed with them. So I learned to factor our invoices, and access the cash we needed to further invest in research and development and growth.

- Choose your investors carefully. Not all money is good money, even when it comes from reputable venture capitalists. Align your vision and culture with your financial partner, your venture capitalists. The wrong relationship will be a loss–loss right off the bat. My standard for managing my venture capital risk was always to look for "high-octane" money.
- Seeking growth capital may require accepting a substantial risk and sharing your destiny with a board of directors. The worst risk for an entrepreneur, from my perspective, is accepting money from what seems to be a great investor group and inheriting "green" MBA analysts to sit on one's board. My risk tolerance for board members has always been low, and I have established a clear set of criteria for accepting a board member, which I would recommend to other entrepreneurs. Potential board members:
  1. Must have built and operated a business of their own – they must have been entrepreneurs.
  2. Must share your values and philosophy and show genuine care and empathy for people.
  3. Must have pockets that are deep enough and an appetite big enough to invest in multiple rounds, because you will always underestimate how much you really need.

Looking back, I am glad that I decided I would take a more active role in managing the risks associated with my professional and financial life. I have been blessed with a fabulous life. Genny and I have been married for 25 years; we have three great kids; and together we have traveled the world. In the process I have built three businesses, and I am thankful to have received Morton's advice as I built each one.

The first business was the most adventurous, but did not succeed (but we drank a lot of vodka!). The second venture secured our financial success. My third business, which Deloitte named one of the "top ten hottest startups in the New York area," grew into a global learning technology leader, and was recently acquired by one of the largest enterprise software firms in the world. Not only did the buyout send a couple of coins into my pockets, but also it resulted in the acquiring company's CEO asking me to stay on and build a new game – changing global business.

Morton's book covers a broad stretch of material, ranging from how banks evaluate a loan application to how a business's worth is evaluated. *Navigating the Business Loan* reads smoothly, not like the usual technical texts about small and mid-sized businesses. In this book I discovered ways managers can fine-tune business plans by effortlessly entering forecast equations (the ones banks typically employ) directly into cell phones or tablets; now we can punch keys to ascertain financial needs, calculate sales growth rates that call for external financing, and perform other loan calculations. If you give this book to your accountant, he or she can develop a "banker's cash flow" from scratch, step by step. I would say that the chapters on cell phone and tablet entries and cash flow construction alone are an important contribution to the literature on small and mid-sized business, and make *Navigating the Business Loan* well worth its price. I only wish Morton had written this terrific book much earlier.

Ara Ohanian

COMPANION WEBSITE

A companion website with supplementary material can be found at:
http://booksite.elsevier.com/9780128016985

CHAPTER 1

Business Structures and Funding Sources*

While traditionally small firms have established relationships with commercial banks, the era of easy credit is over. With many large banks now partially owned by the government, and with toxic loans still on the books, you may discover that banks are not as friendly to small business as they once were. So what do you do if you need capital for your business right now? The good news is that there are still options out there; banks are not the only shops in town. You may need to look in new places and be creative to find low-cost money to start or expand your business. Just one caveat – to get the most bang for the buck, you must be exceptionally prepared as you talk over financing requirements. This book should help you open a few doors.

While it is true that the era of easy credit for small businesses is past, viable businesses that qualify for credit can take advantage of historically low interest rates and an increasingly robust lending environment. If you are prepared to argue your business's merits with confidence, if you understand the inner workings of lenders' operations, if you are hands-on in meeting lenders' requirements, and if you can perform the due diligence processes offered in this book, bank and other cheap credit sources can be yours.

---

*Please visit http://booksite.elsevier.com/9780128016985 to view the ancillary material of this chapter.

Navigating the Business Loan. http://dx.doi.org/10.1016/B978-0-12-801698-5.00001-7

So how can you take advantage of emerging ease of access to credit, which will allow you not only to finance your business with cheap funds but also to build a sustainable relationship with your lender? First, you will need to understand the inner workings of credit risk due diligence as it applies to your business, which is clarified in this book. Follow up by initiating communications. Your attorneys and accountants can help facilitate this, perhaps during a business lunch. If you are not yet a customer, convince potential lenders to set up a solicitation folder that will hold records of on-site calls, business discussions, and financial figures.

Remember, bankers have high loan approval criteria; their standards fall within the institution's credit policy and procedure guidelines. Today, the name of the game is adequate client information, sophisticated analytic tools, banker-styled cash flows, business and equity valuations, computer risk modeling, simulation analytics, stochastic optimization, and interactive credit risk ratings. *Why now and not before?* Because the debt crisis showed lenders insisting on "know thy customer" that due diligence spelled the difference between successful, survivable banking and chaotic, lax infrastructures that contributed to the demise of many once-proud financial institutions. Narrowly focused and ill-informed banking primed to attract loan volume at the expense of quality is a thing of the past.

In this chapter, we will review common small-business structures and lending sources, go over the steps you should take before arranging a loan interview, and list the documentation required to apply for a small-business loan.

SHORT REVIEW OF BUSINESS STRUCTURES

Here are some questions lenders ask when they evaluate a small business's prospects for success. Keep these questions in mind as we review common small-business types and their associated risks.

- Are opportunities sought in the marketplace viable for future growth?
- Is the company's structure feasible, given the direction and resources available?
- Does the company operate with a well-defined, feasible business plan?

- Can the company eventually compete in global markets?
- How good are the leadership qualities of people running the operation?
- What phase of the business cycle is the company in?
- Which loan product would be optimal?

Family-owned, small, and entrepreneurial businesses in general: Family-controlled businesses typically represent a market segment in which financial service needs are great. Small- to middle-market businesses provide bankers with opportunities to offer advice on expansion, estate planning, financial asset management, and consulting. These opportunities can result not only in maintaining operating accounts for the business, but also in opening personal accounts for family members. This arrangement improves the bank's operating balances for the current period, as well as the present value of all future balances.

Often, family businesses are passed down from one generation to the next. In the past, leadership roles automatically devolved to the eldest son. Now, management control tends to be more widely distributed and business owners generally are willing to seek help in making these choices. Still, sometimes family businesses lack definitive direction due to ill-prepared succession management and difficulties resulting from family members working together. These situations may lead family-run businesses to be unaware of the early stages of financial difficulties, or to ignore financial distress signals. Often management is unable to cope with a crisis because ownership is not separate from management; there might be no perceived fiduciary duty if management is not separated from ownership. In some cases, owner-managers inherit the wealth, but not the skills and talents of prior management. Sometimes management fails to properly train the heir-apparent. For example, the CEO may have far too many expectations of his or her successor, yet resist training the successor or bringing in competent management from outside the company.

Typical small-to-middle-market, family-run businesses are also more prone to financial crises than other types of firms, particularly during transitional phases between generations. Small businesses may have neither the assets nor the infrastructure to withstand recessions and other unforeseen economic disruptions. Without the manpower and expertise of larger companies, they are more susceptible to failure. Here are some warning signals that indicate that all is not well in a small business:

- A decline in operating margins and/or a loss of working capital. These problems, if not addressed, could turn a short-term cash shortfall into a severe liquidity crisis.
- Overly optimistic sales forecasts. Small businesses may attempt to project good results in an effort to hide financial distress signals.
- Failure to keep pace with changing trends, including customer preferences, new technologies, government regulations, and stiffer competition as the industry matures.
- Inability to submit financial statements in a timely manner. Typically the accountant's opinion letter should not be dated more than 90 days past the fiscal year-end.
- Process slowdowns attributable to failing equipment as management elects to forego costs involved with maintaining existing equipment and/or replacing obsolete equipment. Most severe financial problems in family-run businesses occur within a year of starting operations.
- As the burden on cash flow is increased, the company may try to increase sales through any means possible. These attempts might include price-cutting and deal-making. Sales may be made to customers with poor credit ratings, which will result in collecting problems. As assets become tied up in outstanding receivables, additional strain is placed on cash flow. As a result, the firm might not be able to meet its short-term needs, so trade debt will build up while the company can still get credit.

While small-business owners are risk-takers, they are nevertheless also innovative and creative visionaries attempting to build long-term value, to identify opportunities, and to capitalize on change. Truly exceptional accomplishments in business are the product of small ideas molded by entrepreneurial perspective. Small businesses should not be viewed as short-term propositions, but as serious long-term prospects. Successful pioneers such as Sam Walton, Steven Jobs, and Ray Kroc were all entrepreneurs who harnessed small ideas and converted them into large, profitable corporations.

Sole proprietorship: Sole proprietorships are the simplest and most common structure chosen to start a business. It is an unincorporated business owned and run by one individual with no distinction between the business and the owner. As the owner, you are entitled to all profits and are responsible for all your business's debts, losses, and liabilities. You do not have to take any formal action to form a sole proprietorship. As long as you are the only owner, this status automatically comes from your business activities. In fact, you may already own one without knowing it. If you are a freelance writer, for example, you are a sole proprietor. But like all businesses, you need to obtain the necessary licenses and permits. Because you and your business are one and the same, the business itself is not taxed separately. Keep in mind the downsides of sole proprietorship (your lender will!):

1. Unlimited personal liability: Because there is no legal separation between you and your business, you can be held personally liable for the debts and obligations of the business. This risk extends to any liabilities incurred as a result of employee actions.
2. Difficulty raising money: Because you can't sell stock in the business, there is little opportunity for investment. Banks are also hesitant to lend to a sole proprietorship because of a perceived lack of repayment options if the business fails.
3. Pressure: The flip side of complete control is the heavy burden and pressure it can impose. You alone are ultimately responsible for the successes and failures of your business.

Partnership: A partnership is a single business in which two or more people share ownership. Each partner contributes to all aspects of the business, including money, property, labor, or skill. In return, each partner shares the profits and losses of the business. Because partnerships entail more than one person in the decision-making process, your lender will want to review the partnership agreement. The agreement should document how future business decisions will be made, including how the partners will divide profits, resolve disputes, change ownership (bring in new partners or buy out current partners), and dissolve the partnership.

There are three general types of partnership arrangements. *General partnerships* assume that profits, liability, and management duties are divided equally among partners. If you opt for an unequal distribution, the percentages assigned to each partner must be documented in the partnership agreement. *Limited partnerships* give partners limited liability as well as limited input with regard to management decisions. These limits depend on the extent of each partner's investment percentage.

Limited partnerships are attractive to investors in short-term projects. *Joint ventures* act like general partnerships, but exist for only a limited time period or for a single project. Partners in a joint venture can be recognized to be in an ongoing partnership if they continue the venture, but they must file as such.

Be wary of partnership's possible pitfalls. Like sole proprietorships, partnerships retain full, shared liability among the owners. Partners are not only liable for their own actions but also for the business debts and decisions made by other partners. In addition, the personal assets of all partners can be used to satisfy the partnership's debt. With multiple partners, disagreements are bound to happen. Partners should consult each other on all decisions, make compromises, and resolve disputes as amicably as possible. Unequal contributions of time, effort, or resources can cause discord among partners.

Sub S corporations: Probably the most notable difference between an S corporation and a regular C corporation is that the S corporation is generally not subject to federal income tax. Its net taxable income is reported by the stockholders of the S corporation on a pro rata basis, and added to their other income or losses on their personal federal income tax returns. Some of the disadvantages of S corporations are that they cannot deduct expenses unless or until actually paid to stockholders, and they are limited in their ability to deduct certain fringe benefits of shareholders (e.g., health insurance). Also, income is taxed to top shareholders even if it is not distributed. As far as lenders are concerned, if tax liabilities are imposed on the stockholders of an S corporation, it may be necessary to distribute funds from the corporation to the stockholders for the payment of these taxes. Lenders are concerned with whether or not this is in the corporation's and stockholders' best interests. A fully taxable corporation paying its income taxes is part of the normal course of business and even the most conservative lender would not try to restrict this. A lender will ask, "Which approach will result in the lowest overall tax payment: a direct tax payment by a taxable corporation or a distribution by an S corporation to its stockholders?" When S status is elected because the tax liability is less, the lender benefits by having a financially stronger customer.

Franchises: Why have banks kept their distance from the franchise industry? Many obstacles that franchisees and their parent companies encounter relate to the local dispositions of many of the United States regional banks. Even banks that have long, successful relationships with companies balk at lending across state lines to franchise a product or service. What is more, the same company may be unable to find banks willing to support its franchise-based expansion in any state. In general, this reluctance relates in part to poor understanding of how the franchise business operates. The success of franchising is correlated to several factors, one of which is the ongoing relationship between franchiser and franchisee. The franchiser's commitment to exporting expertise in marketing, production, and distribution to the franchisee is critically important. The credit analysis of a franchise deal is a double-edged sword, covering both the national–local partnership, which means credentials and personal finances are carefully scrutinized. Credit analysis related to the franchisee includes a detailed financial history and chronicle of skills brought to the business. Lenders must be comfortable with the franchisee's personal credit score, personal net worth, management ability, education, track record, and reputation in the community. Since extensions of credit will likely be secured by collateral, the lender may ask for an interest in the assets, including real estate holdings. Liquid assets are particularly sought after because franchises are rarely profitable in the initial stage, often requiring periodic cash infusions over the course of the loan.

Virtual corporations: A virtual corporation is a temporary alliance of independent companies such as suppliers, customers, and rival businesses, who share skills, profits, and expenses while introducing new goods and services to the marketplace. It can exist without a central office, hierarchy, or vertical integration. The key to its success is simply the formation of a partnership. Virtual corporations exist for two main reasons: (1) the majority of existing companies are unable to introduce products quickly enough in ever-changing global markets, and (2) start-ups usually lack the capital or desire to build an organization from the ground up. Apple and Compaq have thrived on this concept for years at the expense of their competitors. Smaller companies take advantage of outsourcing to maintain flexibility, cash flow, and low overhead. The bottom line is that virtual corporations can be a very profitable way of doing business for all parties concerned. Banks involved in virtual corporations not only benefit from their success but also build relationships with all the players involved. This can have a multiplier effect on future business as old virtual corporations are disbanded and new ones established. From the bank's perspective, the key is prudent credit judgment with regard to all parties involved.

Cooperatives: A cooperative is a business or organization owned by and operated for the benefit of those using its services. Cooperatives are common in the healthcare, retail, agriculture, art, and restaurant industries. Profits and earnings generated by the cooperative are distributed among its members, also known as user-owners. Typically, an elected board of directors and officers run the cooperative, whereas regular members have voting power to control the direction of the cooperative. Members can become part of the cooperative by purchasing shares, though the number of shares they hold does not affect the weight of their votes. If members do not fully participate and perform their duties, including voting or carrying out daily operations, then the business cannot operate at full capacity, and if lack of participation becomes an ongoing issue for a cooperative, it risks losing members. Cooperatives may suffer from slower cash flow since members' incentive to contribute depends on how much they use the cooperative's services and products. While the one member-one vote philosophy is appealing to small investors, larger investors may choose to invest their money elsewhere because a larger share of investment in a cooperative does not grant greater decision-making power.

SELECTING A FINANCING SOURCE

To stand the best chance of succeeding with your loan application, approach a financial institution that is familiar with your industry and target market. Your local chamber of commerce, small business development center, or other business networking group should be able to point you in the right direction. You may also benefit from approaching smaller community banks, as opposed to the larger national banks because they can often put a face to the application process, and since they operate locally, there is a good chance that they will have prior knowledge of your business.

Commercial banks: Choosing a bank involves more than locating a branch a few blocks away. You need to take note of services you require and those services' cost. You want a banker who will take the time to understand your business, help solve problems, and recommend optimum financing so that you can focus on your business. Unfortunately, some business owners spend more time bargain hunting for a printer than shopping for a bank. Rates charged by large financial institutions tend to be lower than those charged by smaller ones. Larger banks are also more likely to issue corporate credit cards to small businesses, which can be used for financing. Find out if your bank is comfortable working with the US Small Business Administration (SBA). Federally subsidized loans help protect the bank against default, which offers an essential motive to lend if credit histories, cash flows, or collateral would be inadequate for a small business to obtain traditional bank loans. Larger banks are likely to make loans backed by the SBA, which allow them accept riskier borrowers.

Notwithstanding tighter lending policies and procedures, commercial banks generally offer added benefits, particularly cutting-edge online services like tax and accounting assistance, direct deposit, invoices, collections, and payroll. A sample of small-business banking needs offered at commercial banks includes checking accounts, business savings accounts, credit cards, deposit-only cards, discounted employee checking accounts, online banking, lines of credit, term loans, equipment leasing, SBA loans, wire transfers, wholesale lockboxes, merchant services, import/export, payroll, retirement accounts, and insurance.

Community banks: Lower fees and higher savings rates are a few advantages of smaller, local banks. As large banks tighten credit and raise fees, community banks have become more attractive. Small banks have been known to be more lenient when considering customers' financial needs and will consider your application as a whole rather than funnel personal data and credit reports through a programmed system. Smaller, regionally focused banks know local market conditions. They often provide more one-on-one access to a loan officer and put more emphasis on a borrower's character rather than applying a credit-score model. And they can be more flexible during tough times, covering overdrawn accounts without imposing stiff penalties. Customer service has become the trademark at local banks, making it less likely that you will pay for personalized care. Deposit rates are likely to be higher, which, along with rewards business checking accounts, can help you survive the low-rate environment. Relationship managers at community-based banks often have more discretion than those at a unit of a big institution and they may consider small-business lending to be their bread and butter.

Lately, however, the distinctions between large and small banks have blurred with the industry's consolidation. Many community banks have undergone mergers that now allow them to offer a wider range of services than in the past. Banks of all sizes are emphasizing improved customer service, having discovered that many customers still prefer face-to-face service at branches than conducting all transactions online. You should compare services between local banks in your community and branches of the major banks to measure what each is willing to offer you and at what price.

Small Business Administration Loans: The SBA provides a number of financial assistance programs for small businesses, including debt financing, surety bonds, and equity financing. The SBA does not make direct loans but instead provides guidelines for loans, which are approved by lenders. The SBA guarantees that loans will be repaid, thus removing lender exposure risk. So when a business applies for an SBA loan, it is actually applying for a commercial loan, structured according to SBA requirements with an SBA guarantee. However, SBA-guaranteed loans may not be in the cards if your business has access to other financing sources offering reasonable terms. The SBA participates in a number of loan programs designed for business owners who may have problems qualifying for a traditional bank loan. To start the process, you should visit a local bank or lending institution that participates in SBA programs. SBA loan applications are structured to meet SBA requirements, so that the loan is eligible for an SBA guarantee. This guarantee represents the portion of the loan that the SBA will repay to the lender if you default on your loan payments.

Credit unions: Credit unions are nonprofit organizations that have two goals: (1) provide services at lower cost, and (2) spread proceeds among members, or those who participate in the credit union, its customers. As traditional financial institutions create more complex lending policies, more businesses are leaning toward alternative funding sources. Most credit unions offer the same services and products that banks do, including mortgages, competitive interest rates, lines of credit, auto loans, lower balance requirement checking and savings accounts, the convenience of electronic banking, and ATMs. Credit unions usually have less rigid loan requirements than commercial banks.

Angel investors: Angel investors are private investors who finance small firms in exchange for equity ownership. Angel investors generally do not expect quick returns and will consider small loans payable over longer periods. Equity financing relieves business of having to repay investors, but angel investors may take on a substantial management role. Many angel investors are dedicated to helping the business succeed, rather than making an enormous return. Angel investors and venture capitalists are diametrically opposed as far as profit motivations are concerned.

Asset-based financing: Asset-based financing is secured by collateral, such as accounts receivable, inventory, equipment, or real estate, which provides structured working capital and term loans. Many lenders prefer to collateralize receivables due their relatively quick turnover. The big advantage of this funding alternative is ownership equity retention. This type of financing is best for start-up companies, refinancing loans, and management buy-ins/outs.

Purchase order financing: Purchase order financing is an option to fill single or multiple customer orders. There will be times when cash is unavailable to fulfill an order. Having to turn the order down could mean revenue loss and perhaps diminished trust, because potential customers who are considering doing business may think twice. Therefore, to avoid such damaging scenarios, it is imperative that firms, especially new firms, find funding to complete orders.

Equipment leasing: Equipment financing saves working capital that would otherwise be used if you were to pay cash for your equipment. With an equipment lease program, the lessee makes affordable monthly payments over time. This allows you to save your money for business expenses and expansion and offers attractive tax benefits. Lease payments are fully tax-deductible if your business uses the leased equipment. When you buy equipment, you are committed to it unless you can sell it. So, if your business uses equipment that is periodically updated with better technology and capabilities, leasing might be the best financing option. Being able to make upgrades to newer equipment when your short-term lease expires can give your company a competitive edge.

Equipment leasing allows businesses to keep credit lines open and enhances cash flow.

Factoring: Your firm's accounts receivables are sold at a discount to a factor, freeing up cash. Factoring receivables on a no-recourse basis means the factor assumes collection responsibility. This kind of funding requires no financial information and is usually quick, but fees charged by most factoring companies are higher than interest on loans.

Credit cards: Owners who depend on credit cards enjoy as-needed access to credit and a good way to build up a rock-solid credit history for future loans. Make sure you are able to pay off large balances and shop for a card with the lowest interest rate. Be wary because some providers may offer a very low initial interest rate that quickly jumps by several percentage points once the introductory period ends. And be careful: one late payment may result in a big increase in rates.

Venture capital: Investors – individual or a small group – who require a high return secured by a substantial ownership stake in a business are venture capitalists. The loans are often expensive, carrying rates of up to 30% annual rate of return. Unlike banks and other lenders, venture capitalists usually take equity positions, meaning you do not have to pay out debt service (interest and principal installments), but instead must surrender a large portion of your company to get financing.

Venture capitalists invest in start-up or early-stage, high-growth small firms in exchange for a portion of the company they anticipate being sold to the public or to larger firms within a few years' time. These firms generally have proprietary new technologies, dominant positions in emerging markets, strong management, and the potential to be acquired by a larger company or to be taken public in a stock offering. There are several types of venture capitalists, including private venture capital partnerships that search for businesses with the capability to generate a 30% annual return. Industrial venture capital pools focus on firms with high potential for success, such as high-tech, innovative operations using state-of-the-art know-how in a distinctive way.

Crowd-funding: Crowd-funding refers to the collective cooperation, attention, and trust of people who network and pool their money and other resources together to support efforts initiated by other people or organizations. The purpose of crowd-funding varies, from disaster relief to citizen journalism to artists seeking support from fans, to political campaigns.

Peer-to-peer lending: Peer-to-peer lending is a method of debt financing that enables individuals to borrow and lend money without the use of an official financial institution as an intermediary. Peer-to-peer lending removes the middleman from the process, but it also involves more time, effort, and risk than the general brick-and-mortar lending scenarios.

Merchant cash advance: Merchant cash advance companies provide funds to businesses in exchange for a percentage of daily credit card income directly from the processor that clears and settles the credit card payment. Most providers form partnerships with card-payment processors and take payments directly from a business owner's card-swipe terminal. The advances are not loans, but rather a sale of a portion of future credit card and/or debit card sales.

Community Development Financial Institution (CDFI): A CDFI is a specialized financial institution that works in market niches that are poorly supported by mainstream financial institutions. CDFIs provide financing and services in economically distressed target markets, such as mortgage financing for low-income and first-time homebuyers and not-for-profit developers; flexible underwriting and risk capital for needed community facilities; and technical assistance, commercial loans, and investments to small start-up or expanding businesses in low-income areas.

Small Business Innovation Research Grants: The SBIR program is a competitive program that encourages domestic small businesses to engage in federal research and development that has the potential for commercialization. Through an awards-based program, small businesses explore their technological potential and are provided the incentive to profit from this technology's commercialization. By including qualified small businesses in R&D, high-tech innovation is stimulated and the government gains entrepreneurial spirit as it meets its specific research and development needs.

Royalty financing: Royalty-based growth capital is increasingly considered an attractive alternative for funding expansion-stage companies, providing capital in exchange for a fixed percentage of future revenue (royalty). A firm pays the royalty monthly until its total payments reach a cap that is expressed as a multiple of the investment amount. This financing alternative preserves ownership, requires no personal guarantees or valuations, and inhibits equity dilution.

Vendor credit: A loan from one company to another that is used to buy goods from the company providing the loan is a vendor credit. The vendor increases sales, earns interest, and may sometimes acquire an interest in the customer.

Home equity loans: A home equity loan is a type of loan in which the borrower uses the equity of his or her home as collateral. Home equity loans are often used to finance small businesses, major expenses such as home repairs, medical bills, or college education. A home equity loan creates a lien against the borrower's house and reduces actual home equity. Most home equity loans require good to excellent credit history, and reasonable loan-to-value and combined loan-to-value ratios.

WHAT TO CONSIDER BEFORE YOU APPLY

Review Credit Reports

Before you apply for commercial credit, you should review your business's credit report, if your business has been in existence for a while. You can obtain a free Business Information Report on your own business from Dun & Bradstreet. If D&B does not yet have any information on your business, they will allow you to voluntarily obtain a listing by providing them with some basic information about your business. Most conventional lenders will expect a minimum of four or five trade experiences listed on a business report before they consider creditworthiness. If you have been operating your business without credit, or with personal assets, you should consider making some trade credit purchases in order to establish a credit history for your enterprise.

Reviewing your consumer credit history is also a must. Consumer credit agencies are required to remove any information from your report that cannot be verified or has been shown to be inaccurate. However, before you submit a letter disputing any debt to the credit reporting company, it may be a good idea to contact the creditor directly. If an error was made, you can often clear up the dispute more quickly if you take the initiative instead of waiting for your lender to point the error out. If the dispute is not resolved and your credit report is not adjusted, you have the right to file a statement or explanation regarding the alleged debt with the credit report. Check your credit score, too. FICO is the most commonly used credit scoring system used in the United States. The score is determined based on five variables: (1) money you owe, (2) types of credit you have obtained, (3) new credit, (4) length of credit history, and (5) payment history. A score of less than 640 is a very low score and can mean you will struggle to obtain credit, and if credit is approved, be prepared to pay high rates. A reasonable score is 641 to 680, but you will probably pay higher-than-average interest rates. A good score of 681 to 720 is associated with credit availability and attractive interest rates. A score above 721 is an excellent credit score. Creditors will want you as a customer and will offer low interest rates.

Prepare a SWOT Matrix

It is a good idea to prepare a SWOT matrix before you finalize a business plan or arrange for a loan interview. A SWOT matrix is a structured planning method to evaluate the strengths, weaknesses, opportunities, and threats associated with your business. A SWOT matrix helps set achievable goals for your organization and shows your lender that you are on top of your business.

S = Strengths: characteristics of your business that give it an advantage over others. What advantages does your organization have over competitors? Are there lowest-cost resources you can draw upon that others cannot? Consider changes in technology and markets on both a broad and narrow scale and changes in government policy related to your business.

W = Weaknesses: characteristics that place the business at a disadvantage relative to others. What could you improve? What should you avoid? What factors lose you sales?

O = Opportunities: features your organization or project could exploit to its advantage: changes in technology and markets, government policy or regulations, legislation, local and global events, and potential new uses of products and services.

T = Threats: industry demographics that could cause trouble in your business. Examples include product obsolescence, new market entrants, and changes in customer tastes.

Check for Red Flags

Here are scenarios virtually all lenders fear. If any of the following applies to your business, have a good explanation ready before you meet with your lender.

- Bookings significantly down compared to benchmarks or industry standard
- Negative trends: losses, weak gross margins, slowness in accounts receivable, and decrease in sales volume
- Intercompany payables/receivables are not adequately explained
- Cash balances reduced substantially or are overdrawn and uncollected during normally liquid periods; management fails to take trade discounts because of poor inventory turnover; low probabilities operating cash flows will cover debt service
- Withholding tax liability builds as taxes are used to pay other debt;
- Frequent downtiering of financial reporting sparked by an effort to bring on a more liberal accountant
- At the end of the cycle, creditors are not completely paid out
- A sharp reduction in officers' salaries brings a lower standard of living at home, and might suggest a last-ditch effort to save a distressed business
- Erratic interim results signaling a departure from normal and historical seasonal patterns
- Financials submitted late in an attempt by management or their accountants to postpone unfavorable news
- Unwillingness to provide budgets, projections, or interim information
- Suppliers cut back terms or request cash on delivery (COD)
- Changes in inventory, followed by an excessive inventory buildup or the retention of obsolete merchandise; the borrower changes suppliers frequently, or transient buying results in higher raw material costs; increased inventory to one customer or perilous reliance on one account; changing concentration from a major well-known customer to one of lesser stature, pointing to problem inventory

- Obligor loses an important supplier or customer; concentrations in receivables and payables along with the failure to obtain satisfactory explanations on concentrations; failure to investigate the credit-worthiness of large receivables
- Intangible signals such as failure to look the banker in the eye, letting the condition of the business premises deteriorate, or taking longer to return calls
- Merchandise shipped out at year-end to window-dress financials; shifting sales to future periods via reserves; income-smoothing gimmicks; creating gains and losses by employing devious gimmicks; hiding losses inside discontinued operations
- Shifting current expenses to later periods by improperly capitalizing costs; amortizing costs too slowly and failing to write off worthless assets; income contributing less and less to overall financing
- Dividends large in proportion to net income
- Related-party or insider receivables; slow receivables turnover (annualized frequently); unreasonable right of return exists on goods shipped
- Unjustified LIFO to FIFO changes
- Insufficient insurance
- Inclusion of inflation profits in inventory
- Bad gross profit trends but no inventory markdowns apparent
- Outdated equipment and technology evidenced by high maintenance and repair expense, declining output level, inadequate depreciation charge, lengthening depreciation period, large write-off of assets, and, especially important, substantial buildup in work-in-process inventory and order backlogs because outdated equipment fails to produce finished goods shipped to customers on a timely basis
- Factory operating well below capacity
- Changes in the manner payables are paid
- Loans to or from officers and affiliates
- Management unclear what condition the company is in and the direction in which it is headed
- Lender fails to interpret the cash budget correctly and as a result overestimates seasonal peaks and valleys, thereby approving an excessive loan
- Unusual items on financial statements
- Changes in financial management (perhaps a revolving door of CFOs as they see the writing on the wall)

- Totals on receivables and payables aging schedules do not agree with amounts shown on the balance sheet of the same date
- Lender approves advances ostensibly to finance a seasonal loan while funds are used for other purposes, notably payments on the bank's own term debt; term debt is handled as agreed, but seasonal advance goes up and stays up
- Lender finances highly speculative inventory with which the borrower is trying for a home run

DOCUMENTATION GENERALLY REQUIRED FOR A SMALL BUSINESS LOAN APPLICATION

While every loan program has specific forms to fill out and documents to submit, you will likely need to submit much of the same information for different loan packages. Before you start applying for loans, you should get some basic documentation together. The following are typical items that will be required to support small business loan applications.

1. *Personal Background: Either as part of the loan application or as a separate document, you will probably be asked to provide some personal background information, including previous addresses, names used, criminal record, educational background, etc.*
2. *Resumes: Some lenders require evidence of management or business experience, particularly for loans that will be used to start a new business.*
3. *Business Plan: All loan programs require a sound business plan to be submitted with the loan application. The business plan should include a complete set of projected financial statements, including profit and loss, cash flow, and a balance sheet. Make sure to prepare a business plan after finalizing a SWOT matrix.*
4. *Personal Credit Report: Your lender will obtain your personal credit report as part of the application process. However, you should obtain a credit report from all three major consumer credit rating agencies before submitting a loan application to the lender. Inaccuracies and blemishes on your credit report can hurt your chances of getting a loan approved. It is critical you try to clear these up before beginning the application process.*
5. *Business Credit Report: If you are already in business, you should be prepared to submit a credit report for your business. As with the personal credit report, it is important to review your business's credit report before beginning the application process.*
6. *Income Tax Returns: Most loan programs require applicants to submit personal and business income tax returns for the previous three years.*
7. *Financial Statements: Many loan programs require owners with more than a 20% stake in a business to submit signed personal financial statements.*

You may also be required to provide projected financial statements either as part of, or separate from, your business plan. It is a good idea to have these prepared and ready in case a program for which you are applying requires these documents to be submitted individually.

8. *Bank Statements: Many loan programs require one year of personal and business bank statements to be submitted as part of a loan package.*

9. *Collateral: Collateral requirements vary greatly. Some loan programs do not require collateral. Loans involving higher risk factors for default require substantial collateral. Strong business plans and financial statements can help you avoid putting up collateral. In any case, it is a good idea to prepare a collateral document that describes the value of personal or business property that will be used to secure a loan.*

10. *Legal Documents: Depending on a loan's specific requirements, your lender may require you to submit one or more legal documents. Make sure you have the following items in order, if applicable:*

    a. *Business licenses and registrations required for you to conduct business*

    b. *Articles of Incorporation*

    c. *Copies of contracts you have with any third parties*

    d. *Franchise agreements*

    e. *Commercial leases*

Source: the Small Business Administration.[1]

When you meet with a lender to request a business loan, present a positive, professional demeanor at the interview. Be prepared for a variety of questions and make sure you can back up all your loan application claims with facts, figures, and navigation tips this book offers. You are selling yourself, your confidence in your business plan, and your ability to make good on your loan. Communicate clearly how much money you need, what you intend to use it for, and exactly where the business loan will be allocated (premises vs. equipment vs. staff vs. other expenditures). Prepare your repayment plan and be sure to include it in your documentation.

---

[1] SBA.Gov, SBA General Small Business loans. 7(a) Loan Application Checklist, updated as of August 2014, http://www.sba.gov/content/sba-loan-application-checklist; 2014.

CHAPTER 2

How Banks Evaluate Your Loan Application*

OUTLINE

What is the overall credit philosophy of financial institutions? Lenders require not only a sense of caution as they move on from the debt crisis but also the courage and wisdom to take reasonable risks. Financial institutions succeed as long as the risks they assume are prudent and remain within clearly defined parameters of portfolio objectives. This means enacting policies and procedures; ensuring that exposures are properly

---

*Please visit http://booksite.elsevier.com/9780128016985 to view the ancillary material of this chapter.

Navigating the Business Loan. http://dx.doi.org/10.1016/B978-0-12-801698-5.00002-9

identified, monitored, and controlled; and making sure that loan pricing, terms, and other safeguards against non-performance or default are commensurate with levels of risk that banks commit to. In short, banks are in the business of making loans, which is what banking is all about.

It is your credit officer's job to use his or her judgment and technical skills, along with the lender's standards for credit analysis, to realize this objective and to ensure your loan request falls within established policy and procedure parameters. For example, reviewing your financial statements may provide your lender with preliminary findings, but that review falls short of assessing the multiplicity of variables that determine your suitability for a loan. It is far more important for a loan officer to master the information necessary to form an opinion than to simply crunch numbers.

What if a loan officer determines that your business financing expectations exceed his or her ability to satisfy the loan? Does this suggest that all possible sources of repayment have been exhausted? No, but it is up to you to state your position's merits. Since your banker's key objective is to increase profitability by exercising sound credit judgment, show clearly and confidently how your business plan fits the bill, particularly in key areas like loan repayment and protection.

Since lenders are in the business of taking calculated risks, why are banks so concerned about losing money on deals like yours? After experiencing the recent financial crunch, your bank can never reasonably price loans at a loss even if the probability of default decreases. For example, if your bank's net interest margin is 4% annually, it would take 25 years to recoup 100% of a loss, not including related overhead costs or the time-value of money. Thus, your banker will zero-in on your debt-paying abilities.

Critical risk assumptions affecting your business play a major role in finalizing lending decisions. You should have a clear understanding of what they are before visiting your lender. A typical credit officer has many questions when you walk through the door: Who runs this business? What is the purpose of this loan? Is this company capable of making repayment in a timely manner? What protection will my bank have against default? Does this all fit nicely into a big picture relating to the exposure's risk/reward profile?

Credit decision making is largely broken into two parts: (1) primary and (2) analytic evaluations. These two components serve as road maps, functioning very much like a GPS. Subsets are analyzed and interpreted before your banker moves to the next lending attribute, just as your GPS takes you to your destination one turn at a time. Essentially, primary and analytic constituents – however small in isolation – build up and move along, much like the decision trees you read about in finance books. In this chapter, we will climb up our credit decision tree, looking at the branches as if they were pieces in a jigsaw puzzle, and with a little work settle on the decision branch – the spot where all the pieces of the loan puzzle fit together.

PRIMARY EVALUATION

Primary evaluation represents broad qualitative, general assessment of an obligor's business.

Business Operations

Certain business attributes provide bankers with an image of their borrowers. Each business type has its own idiosyncrasies. If your firm is made up of different operations, it is important to show your bank the sales and profit contributions for each unit. For example, how are funds allocated to each part of the operation? Say ABC Corporation has appropriated most of its consolidated cash flow to a unit contributing 25% to total sales and only 2% to profits. Smart lenders know that companies in the mature or declining phase of their growth cycle often seek fresh investments to invigorate lackluster business units, often at the bank's expense.

You might begin by reviewing management's strategic goals. Go over the firm's history, including predecessor companies, and follow up with a description of products, markets, principal customers, subsidiaries, and lines of business. Have there been any recent product changes and technological innovation? Prepare a list of principal suppliers, together with approximate annual amounts purchased, noting delinquencies in settlement of suppliers' accounts. Your lender will ask you to provide both the numbers and types of customers broken down by percentage of sales (or profit contribution), noting whether or not you are overdependent on one or a few customers. In addition, distinguish market segmentation by customer type, geographic location, product, distribution channels, pricing policy, and degree of integration. How economically sensitive is the business to new products, competitors, interest rates, and disposable income? Is the company seasonal? How well has your business fared in good and bad markets, compared with the rest of the industry? Finally, what are the firm's capital equipment requirements?

Lenders are concerned with industry failure rates. Therefore, they expect borrowers to know their industries cold. Competitive advantage, industry phase and composition, reliance on exports, trends, and market share are central concerns. The information flow begins with company attributes. Here is a checklist of information you should be prepared to provide your lender:

Company Attributes
- History of the business, including any predecessor companies, changes in capital structure, present capitalization, and any insolvency proceedings
- Description of products, markets, principal customers, subsidiaries, and lines of business
- Recent product changes and technological innovation
- Customer growth, energy availability, and possible ecological problems
- List of the company's principal suppliers, together with approximate annual amounts purchased, noting delinquencies in settlement of suppliers' accounts
- Market segmentation by customer type, geographic location, product-distribution channels, pricing policy, and degree of integration
- Strategic goals and track record meeting or missing goals
- Numbers and types of customers broken down in percentage of sales and profit contribution
- Note the extent the borrower is overdependent on one or a few customers
- Government contracts
- Capital equipment requirements and commitments

Industry Attributes
- Industry composition and recent changes in that composition
- Image of the company and its products and services compared with industry leaders

- Number of firms included in the industry and whether that number has been declining or increasing
- The firm's market share and recent trends
- Recent industry merger, acquisition, and divestiture activities, along with prices paid in these transactions
- Recent foreign entrants to the industry
- Suppliers' versus buyers' power
- Bases of competition
- Industry's rate of business failure
- Industry's average credit rating
- Degree of operating leverage inherent in the industry
- Industry reliance on exports and degree of vulnerability
- Trade organizations, consultants, economists, and security analysts that can help your banker complete cash flow forecasts
- Adverse conditions reported by financial, investment, or industry analysts
- Extent litigation that will affect production or demand for industry's products
- Government regulations and environmental issues and their effect on the industry
- If publicly traded, the exchanges on which the stock is traded, the dealer-making markets for over-the-counter stock, institutional holdings, trading volume, and total market capitalization

Management

Here is a quote from "Principles for the Management of Credit Risk Consultative paper issued by the Basel Committee on Banking Supervision Basel July 1999":

Banks need to understand to whom they are granting credit. Therefore, prior to entering into any new credit relationship, a bank must become familiar with the borrower or counterparty and be confident that they are dealing with an individual or organization of sound repute and creditworthiness. In particular, strict policies must be in place to avoid association with individuals involved in fraudulent activities and other crimes. This can be achieved through a number of ways, including asking for references from known parties, accessing credit registries, and becoming familiar with individuals responsible for managing a company and checking their personal references and financial condition. However, a bank should not grant credit simply because the borrower or counterparty is familiar to the bank or is perceived to be highly reputable.

Who are the key players and what are their respective accountabilities? It is a good idea to prepare brief biographical summaries of your key players. Generally, lenders look for two qualities: (1) management's capacity to effectively guide the firm along bumpy roads and (2) management's willingness to repay during hard times. The key to effective management in turn deals with, again, two qualities: (1) ability to respond to changes in the external environment and (2) ability to creatively deploy internal resources to improve competitive position.

A few words on integrity: Since mainstream information comes from management, lenders must have confidence in that information. The amount and quality of data often depend on the deal's requirements and information management is willing to supply. Consider the following:

- List of officers and directors, along with affiliations, ages, and years in office
- Names, addresses, and contacts of professional advisers, including attorneys, auditors, principal bankers at other banks, and investment bankers
- TRW credit reports, Better Business Bureau, and Dun & Bradstreet ratings
- Number of people employed and major areas of activity
- Approaches to improving market share and profitability
- Examples of management's problem-solving and decision-making abilities (correct decisions made at the appropriate level)
- The work environment
- Instances showing how management and subordinates work as an effective team
- Officer salaries plus constructive profits (travel and entertainment expenses) to net revenues ratio. Match this ratio to that of similar companies in the industry. Is your compensation equitable or are you taking an unreasonable amount out of your business?
- Examples showing how you prevent problems from arising, instead of wasting valuable time to work out the same problems repeatedly
- Reputation of present owners, directors, management, and professional advisers gathered from industry journals, periodicals, and the Internet
- Adequacy of quantitative and statistical information including strategic and tactical plans, effective policies and procedures,

adequate management information systems, budgetary control and responsibility accounting, standards of performance and control, management and manpower development
- Organization chart and business plans, both short- and long-range plans

Experienced bankers can usually tell if business objectives and strategies are genuine or presented for show.

Bank Relationship
If the relationship is an existing one, how solid has it been? Obviously, a loyal customer going back many years receives better treatment than a credit-seeker walking through the door for the first time. Organize and be prepared to reinforce bank relationship selling points such as age of the account, demand deposit balances, loan history, affiliated accounts, mortgages, personal and business investment accounts, and other services.

Financial Reporting
Lenders naturally assess auditors that prepare fiscal statements. Are financials liberal or conservative? Do they provide an accurate picture of the borrower's condition? The following are good pointers:

- Provide audited financial statements, including registration statements (if they exist) and comparative financial results by major division
- Be prepared to supply tax returns for the past 5 years
- Obtain SEC filings and a shareholder list, if available
- Procure recent unaudited quarterly statements including sales backlog information and a description of accounting practices
- Review the adequacy and sophistication of your firm's internal auditing systems
- Be prepared to report on the adequacy of internal accounting controls, especially management controls, making sure earnings were not inappropriately managed
- Assess the strength of the financial management and controllership function
- Think about how often internal reports are issued, how soon after the end of a period reports are available, and if they are used,

whether the internal reporting timetable and content are consistent with your auditor's monthly closing requirements
- Find out whether subsidiaries have autonomous accounting departments that may not be functioning uniformly and, if so, how overall control is exercised

---

Financial reporting watch list typically includes:
1. Excessively liberal accounting
2. Inappropriate provisions for sales returns, obsolete inventories, or contingent liabilities
3. Expenses associated with cash paid to stockholders, directly or through bargain pricing
4. Product liability
5. Lawsuits
6. Pension plan unfunded past service costs
7. Cutbacks in discretionary expenses: advertising, personnel development, and maintenance
8. Stockholder-managers drawing excessive compensation
9. Adoption of less conservative accounting policies
10. Sales subject to warranty and service guarantees
11. Inaccurate interim reports

ANALYTIC EVALUATION

Analytic evaluation consists of both qualitative and quantitative aspects lenders rely on to complete due diligence and make appropriate credit decisions.

Intention (Purpose)

There are three reasons why firms borrow. First, firms borrow to make asset purchases: short-term purchases to finance seasonality and long-term purchases to support growth. Short-term credit lines finance the acquisition of seasonal assets like inventory. Loans are repaid once inventory is worked down and receivables are collected. Term loans of a year or more usually finance fixed assets or non-seasonal current assets.

Second, firms borrow to replace other creditors in the short or long term. For example, a business saves money by borrowing to take advantage of trade discounts. Loan requests to pay off other financial institutions are feasible if your banker offers better rates or service.

Finally, firms borrow to replace equity. Loans might be required for stock buybacks (e.g., buying up a partner's share in the business), acquisitions, leveraged buyouts, or employee stock option plans. Equity replaced by debt can dislodge the debt-to-equity ratio and cash-flow coverage, putting the remaining equity at risk. One reason lenders prepare pro forma (what-if) financial statements is to insure equity is unimpaired.

Repayment

Companies raise money internally through business activities and externally from debt and equity sources. Asset liquidations inject cash as well, but are a secondhand source of money. The conversion/contraction process is associated with short-term internal repayment sources as depicted by Figure 2.1.

Say your company borrows to support its seasonal manufacturing operations. At the high point or most active part of the period, debt and assets increase to support seasonal activity, thus expanding the balance sheet. During this phase, sales emulate the manufacturing cycle, the result of which is the conversion of inventory into accounts receivables. At the low point or least active part of the period, the manufacturing cycle has ebbed, leaving the firm with the responsibility to clean up outstanding short-term debt. This is accomplished through the conversion of accounts receivables to cash or deposits. Once all short-term debt has been satisfied, the firm's balance sheet will contract back to its normal

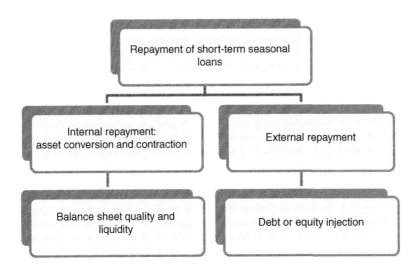

Figure 2.1. Repayment of short-term seasonal loans

low point (fiscal level). Any excess cash on hand is usually designated for temporary current asset investments next season. Thus, the seasonal conversion process becomes the primary source of seasonal debt repayment. Seasonal loans provide for the short-term working capital needs of eligible small businesses by financing seasonal increases in the trading assets (receivables and inventory), the liquidation of which repays the loan at the end of each season. Therefore, it is a self-liquidating loan, its repayment dependent on the conversion of seasonal current assets into cash. The name of the game is both quality and liquidity of the balance sheet.

Creditors know that if a balance sheet fails to fully convert, a company may seek external sources to cover exposures in the form of new outside debt or equity injections. Bankers thus evaluate a borrower's debt capacity. The key attributes lenders consider when firms apply for new monies are the borrower's reputation, existing capital structure, asset quality, profit-generating abilities, and economic value.

Internal repayment of long-term loans, displayed in Figure 2.2, directly relates to historical and projected cash-flow quality, magnitude, and trend. Historical cash-flow analysis provides a track record of the

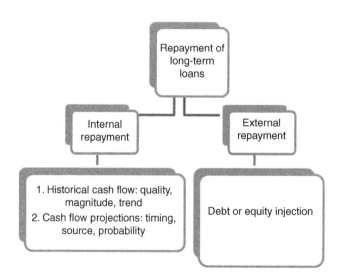

Figure 2.2. Repayment of long-term loans

company's past performance. Can the obligor provide enough cash flow to support asset investment(s)? As for the cash flow itself, how does one evaluate quality, magnitude, and trend? We will cover these issues in Chapter 6, but for now we can state that historical cash flow quality and magnitude are related to an important cash flow grouping called gross operating cash flow (net income plus noncash charges less noncash credits plus nonoperating charges and minus nonoperating credits).

When gross operating cash flow includes lots of fluff – depreciation, deferred taxes, asset write-downs, and extraordinary items – with meager earnings adding little cash, there may not be sufficient cash to repay debt. The magnitude and quality of cash flow in the context of the borrower's growth plans help pinpoint external financing requirements. Usually the weaker the cash flow, the larger the debt needed to support long-term growth plans. If, for example, income is too weak to service debt from one year to the next, a firm could default and possibly go bankrupt. Astute lenders will not advance money to firms that waste assets or that cannot generate enough cash flow to pay down debt. So do your homework, read over Chapter 6, and be familiar with the inner workings of gross operating cash flow.

Cash-flow projections, including timing, source, and probability, represent a second side of internal (long-term) payment (Figure 2.2). Projections are not intended to predict the future perfectly, but to help tell how your business will perform under a variety of situations. Your lender will likely ascribe an expected probability to alternative projections and decide on the scenario that best predicts repayment ability. Keep in mind that projections quantify expectations but will neither replace judgment and experience nor the ability to perceive and distinguish relationships.

Let's look at external repayment of long-term (e.g., cash flow) loans (Figure 2.2). External repayment often depends on whether or not funding sources are readily available. Consider the following:

- What is your firm's debt comfort level?
- Are financial leverage and coverage ratios acceptable?
- To what degree will operating cash flow protect debt service?
- Is asset quality acceptable?
- Can the company sustain its reputation?

Safeguards

What safeguards protect your lender against default? Protection can be internal, external, or a combination of both (see Figure 2.3). Internal protection involves financial analysis, while external protection includes collateral, personal guarantees, and loan covenants. This sounds complicated, but is actually straightforward. Recall that the primary source of internal repayment of short-term loans is balance sheet liquidity, the result of the season's cash conversion cycle, while long-term loans depend on sustained profits and cash flow. Roles are reversed in the safeguards/protection grouping. Seasonal loan (internal) protection is first and foremost a cash flow affair. Your lender wants to make sure a problematic season does not evolve into structural trouble in the years ahead. On the other hand, there is no better protection for long-term loans than a solid, well-capitalized balance sheet. If a business flounders, its resilient balance sheet should be able to delay or even prevent financial distress.

An account of external loan protection follows in the next section.

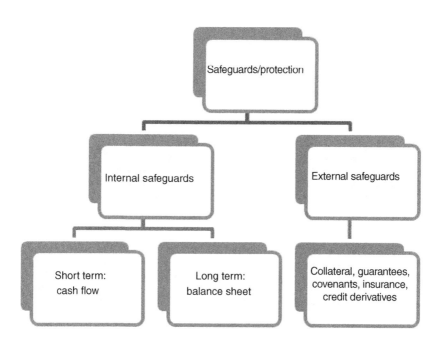

Figure 2.3. Safeguards/protection

Collateral

Collateral is defined as property pledged as security for the satisfaction of a debt or other obligations. Collateral value depends upon, among other things, degree of coverage, economic life cycle of collateral versus term of the loan, possible constraints liquidating collateral, the bank's ability to skillfully and economically monitor collateral, its value against loan exposure, liquidity (how quickly its value may be realized and with what certainty), and of course legal rights.

Guarantees

A guarantee is a written contract, agreement, or undertaking involving three parties: (1) the guarantor agrees to see that the performance of the second party, (2) the guarantee, is fulfilled according to the terms of the contract, agreement, or undertaking, and (3) the creditor, or the party benefiting from the performance.

Loan Covenants

Covenants of a loan agreement lay down the framework for the financial plan jointly agreed upon by the borrower and the lender. The number of covenants and related details depend on the enterprise's financial strength, management's aptitude, and the loan duration.

PERSPECTIVE: HOW LENDERS PUT IT ALL TOGETHER

The decision to approve or decline loans is a three-step process: (1) risk/reward analysis, (2) summary of operating and financing strategies, and (3) finally the outcome itself (decision, alternatives, pricing, default probability, risk-adjusted return on capital, and other matters). Perspective is the spot someplace on the lending decision tree where all the jigsaw puzzle pieces fit together. If you are able to visualize perspective, you are well on your way to appreciating how lenders think. The perspective blueprint follows in three stages.

First Stage: Risk Versus Rewards Analysis

One of the biggest mistakes lenders make is failing to adequately consider a deal's potential risk/reward profile. We saw widespread evidence of slipshod credit decision making prior to the financial crisis. Lenders chased deals fancying the upside while dismissing possibilities of serious erosion in credit quality. The correct line of reasoning behind risk versus reward analysis is that reward (pricing, balances, and relationship) should exceed risk (business failure) by a reasonable margin. The process is of course somewhat subjective. If you were to ask three different lenders to analyze a random company's risk versus reward profile, you would probably get three different responses. However, all lenders ask themselves: What factors within the business reveal the greatest risk? What are our greatest rewards if we foster this relationship by approving the loan?

Many savvy lenders stay ahead of the game by allowing the subjective nature of loan decision making to work to their advantage. They succeed by supplementing experience and know-how with powerful risk versus reward methodologies. Here are two illustrations:

- *Stochastic software:* @ Risk, Crystal Ball, and Risk Simulator use Monte Carlo simulations to depict many possible risk/reward outcomes right in your workbook. Although deterministic optimization problems are formulated with known parameters, real-world dealings like your loan application invariably involve some unknown parameters. This means you can judge which risk undertakings are acceptable and which ones to avoid, allowing for optimal decision making given uncertainty. Stochastic optimization can determine the best allocation of resources, asset balance, and much more.
- *Risk/reward templates[1]:* These templates work by plotting risk along one axis and reward along the other. The four categories are (1) equal low, in which risk and reward are both proportional and low; (2) equal high, in which risk and reward are both proportional and high; (3) positive, representing a positive risk/reward balance, with which a higher return can be expected with limited risk; and (4) negative, denoting a negative risk/reward balance, in which a low return is the reward for taking on a relatively high risk.

Second Stage: Acknowledging the Customer's Strategic Agenda

This stage presents a summary of operating and financing strategies that best realize management's objective which, typically, is to maximize shareholder value

---

[1] Developed by Expert Program Management.

Is the business maximizing shareholder value? Two interrelated value-creating strategies are in play: (1) finance at the lowest sustainable after-tax cost; and (2) allocate capital resources that promise the highest risk-adjusted returns to equity holders. Discounted cash flow valuation, the most frequently used valuation method, provides a going concern value.[2] We determine a firm's value by adding the present value of future cash flows over a discrete forecast horizon (projection period) to the present value of cash flow beyond the forecast horizon (residual or terminal value). We then add unrealized, and/or nonoperating asset values (e.g., unrealized real estate value), the net of the expected value of contingencies. Finally, we derive equity value by subtracting the value of debt from the value of the firm.[3]

Third Stage: Satisfy the Lender's Agenda

A worthy lender's agenda is simply strike an optimal balance between the customer's goal to maximize shareholder value, and the bank's loan approval constraint, placing limits on loss probabilities – a double-edged sword. Will operating and financing goals cause default probabilities to increase beyond a predetermined acceptable level? Internal credit ratings systems help answer this question. Rating systems are at the core of the loan approval process, enabling bankers to spot credit migrations, determine capital allocation, price deals, contribute to profitability analysis, ascertain loan loss reserves, and finally, determine default probability and loss given default. Credit losses are associated with the combined influence of two types of risk factors: those determining whether or not a loan defaults and, in the event of default, risk factors influencing loss rate. Obligor risk that rates key factors is equal to an obligor's default probability, while the facility rating measures risk associated with loan structure. Obligor risk plus facility risk determines loss given default, the most crucial measure in the loan approval process.

Obligor risk involves earnings and operating cash flow, debt capacity and financial flexibility, balance sheet quality and structure, corporate

---

[2] See Chapter 8.
[3] Glantz M, Mun J. The banker's handbook on credit risk: implementing basel II. Chapter 10: The banker's primer on credit risk. Elsevier Academic Press; 2008.

valuation, contingencies, financial reporting, management and controls, industry risk, industry position, and country risk. Facility risk involves documentation, guarantees, collateral, loan purpose, and loan tenor. If you grasp the inner workings of obligor and facility risk, you understand the fundamentals of credit analysis.

The decision: risk rating, defining default probabilities, loss given default and loan loss reserve, recommending pricing and capital allocation.

Question 1: What is the borrower's credit grade[4]?

Lenders visualize your loan request as the probability that exposure loss will be sustained if the credit is approved. Credit risk ratings reflect not only the likelihood or severity of loss, but also the variability of loss over time, particularly as this relates to the effect of the firm's business cycle. Commercial loans expose lenders to two types of risk: (1) obligor risk and (2) facility (or transaction) risk. Obligor risk is associated with economic and industry risks, industry structure risks, customer-specific risks, and the ever-present operating risks inherent in the lending business. These operating risks include earnings and operating cash flow, debt capacity and financial flexibility, balance sheet quality and structure, corporate valuation, contingencies, financial reporting, management and controls, industry risk, industry position, and country risk.

Facility risks are risks inherent in an instrument or facility – documentation, guarantees, collateral, loan purpose, and loan tenor. If your bank feels that combined risk levels are unacceptable, it might sell the exposure or acquire other deals that are less exposed to these forces, thus reducing the risk of its portfolio. Deteriorating corporate grades earn special attention so they can be classified before reaching a point of no return. In addition, credit grades form the basis upon which your bank determines capital and loan loss provisions along with risk-adjusted returns on equity and other key bank benchmarks.

Question 2: What are default probabilities and loss given default associated with your loan application?

---

[4] Glantz M, Kissell R. Multi-asset risk modeling: techniques for a global economy in an electronic and algorithmic trading era, Chapter 10: Rating credit risk: current practices, model design, and applications. Elsevier Academic Press; 2014.

For a high-grade borrower, this risk is small, perhaps one-tenth of 1% per year. For the typical bank borrower this risk is about one-half of 1% annually. While loss probabilities do not seem large, risks can increase quickly and with little warning. All it takes is one major customer taking business elsewhere. Commercial loan margins are tight, and even small default risk miscalculations can undermine your loan's profitability. To complicate matters, financial institutions are themselves borrowers capitalized with high debt (leverage). Unexpected realizations of default risk have destabilized, decapitalized, and destroyed lenders. Banks, finance companies, insurers, investment banks, lessors – none have escaped unscathed.

Default risk cannot be hedged away, or structured away. The government cannot insure it away. It is a reflection of the substantial risk in companies' futures. Various schemes exist, and more are coming, which can shift risk, but in the end, someone must bear this risk. It does not net out in the aggregate. As we saw, loss given default is the combined obligor and facility grades.

Question 3: How do we determine loan loss provision? How do we use it?

Loan loss provisions are expenses set aside as an allowance for bad loans (when a customer defaults, or when terms of a loan must be renegotiated and similar situations). Suppose a bank extends a $500,000, 5-year loan to a restaurant. If the borrower runs into financial problems and currently owes $300,000, the bank will create a loan loss provision. If the bank believes the client will only repay 60% of the borrowed amount, the bank will record a loan loss provision of $120,000 ((100% − 60%) × $300,000).

A notable difference exists between banks following a systematic pricing approach and banks that price *ad hoc*. The rationale for systematic loan pricing is improved risk-adjusted return on equity[5] (RAROC), superior loan yields, better margins, higher fee income, stronger earnings, more efficient credit risk management, and tight customer relationship management. Consistent pricing methodology avoids numerous questionable practices such as failing to factor in default risk, omitting

---

[5] Glantz M, Mun J. Credit engineering for bankers: a practical guide for bank lending. 2nd ed. Chapter 2: Building risk adjusted pricing models. Elsevier Academic Press; 2011.

variable and fixed costs, ignoring cost of funds, and overlooking substantial demand deposits balances. These omissions (pricing errors) encourage firms with weak credit to borrow at the same rates offered to more creditworthy borrowers. Beyond statistical default rates, pricing requires a profound understanding of borrowers along with the ability to judge the qualitative factors on which every risk/return relationship takes root.

Question 4: How should we price this loan?

Due to the nature of this highly competitive business, pricing loans have traditionally been drawn into the so-called relationship parameter. Lending serves as the foundation for broader corporate business, aiming to maximize the profitability of the entire client relationship, rather than focusing on one or two individual loans. As a result, lower deal pricing may be offset by revenue-producing products in other departments (or locales), allowing institutions to earn target returns on a consolidated client basis. In other words, the loan may well serve as the cost of developing broader client relationships. Into the bargain, an effective pricing strategy means developing a price buildup methodology. The methodology works itself through all (pricing) components: obligor risk, facility structure, ancillary costs, global exposure network, and competition.

Question 5: How do we assign a capital allocation to this exposure?

Capital adequacy is a portfolio concept, not usually applicable to individual corporate loans. Banks must have sufficient capital to absorb portfolio extreme (unexpected) losses like unexpected macroeconomic or industry shocks, for example, the 2008 debt crisis. On the other hand, as we saw earlier, individual deals involve measuring expected loss that leads to risk-based provisioning and pricing. Output from portfolio exposure systems is used not just for capital adequacy but also throughout the institution's risk management and incentive systems too. For example, determining break-even prices on credit instruments, setting client exposure limits, deciding on broad portfolio concentration limits, and actively managing overall portfolio credit risk are all part of the day-to-day business of managing the capital structure.

CHAPTER 3

Is Your Financial Information Accurate and Reliable?*

*Please visit http://booksite.elsevier.com/9780128016985 to view the ancillary material of this chapter.

Navigating the Business Loan. http://dx.doi.org/10.1016/B978-0-12-801698-5.00003-0

Few documents are more crucial to lending than good old-fashioned financial statements. In today's tight and selective lending environment, the significance of your auditor's work, that is, the usefulness and credibility of financial statements, cannot be overstated. Through standards adopted by the accounting profession, as well as those imposed both by government and by private business, the accounting profession continues to maintain high standards and improve both the reliability and usefulness of audits. And because properly conducted audits are percussive to credit, and breathe life into the art and science of lending, credit and financial reporting operate as sides of the same coin, like pharmaceuticals research and medical research. Smart lenders do not view financial statements as inanimate, repetitive, or detached objects. After all, financial reports are dynamic.

THE AUDITOR'S ROLE

The auditor's role centers on the preparation of independent reports supported by all tests necessary to verify the reliability and accuracy of the numbers. While financial reports alone are never the sole means of reaching credit decisions, they play a major role within the broader context of lending due diligence because your lender requires a great deal of ancillary information before he or she is comfortable with your business and understands its funding requirements. As we saw in Chapter 2, credit decisions are determined by real values such as the earning power of your firm's assets, never simply on historical financial reports (real values are generally absent from auditors' reports).

Auditors are members of independent accounting firms meeting prescribed professional standards and are licensed to practice in the country or state of their clients. The auditor, on the basis of his or her independent judgment formed against the background of appropriate accounting standards and procedures, attests to the fairness of financial statements presented by management. Auditors are responsible for the proper exercise of judgment in two central areas. They must certify that (1) statements are presented fairly in accordance with generally accepted accounting principles, and (2) adequate disclosure is practiced.

While auditors undertake assignments for fees, it is the accountant's responsibility, not management's (no matter how prodigious the fee), to decide what information, good or bad, is to be disclosed. However, the terms of an accountant's engagement determine to a large degree the extent of audits, number and detail of schedules, and amount of verification work completed. In addition, the adequacy of audits, and the experience and reputation of accountants, is measured against the size and financial condition of borrowers. Accountants have a fiduciary responsibility to clarify auditing data for lenders who request such clarification. If your company is privately owned, your lender may request additional schedules, exhibits, or other information.

Financial reports are expected to present fairly, clearly, and completely the borrower's economic, financial, and operating condition. In preparing financial reports, it is perhaps naïve to think that financial statements are immune to threats of bias, misinterpretation, error, and evasiveness. To minimize these challenges and render financial statements that are industry comparable and period-to-period consistent, the accounting profession developed a body of conventions.

Without accounting conventions, auditors would have to develop a unique theory structure and individualistic set of practices. In this hypothetical and somewhat ridiculous setting, lenders would need to become familiar with each client's anomalous bookkeeping, a nearly impossible task. Thankfully there is almost universal adoption of a common set of accounting concepts, standards, and procedures under the headings of generally accepted accounting principles (GAAP) and international accounting standards (IAS).

Specifically, International Accounting Standards #1 (IAS 1), Disclosure of Accounting Policies, includes the following guidelines for financial reports:

- Fair presentation
- Accounting policies
- Going concern
- Accrual basis of accounting
- Consistency of presentation

- Materiality and aggregation
- Offsetting
- Comparative information

HOW ACCOUNTANTS RECORD TRANSACTION DATA

In view of the basic assumptions of accounting, what are the principles or guidelines that the accountant follows in recording transaction data? The principles relate basically to how assets, liabilities, revenues, and expenses are to be identified, measured, and reported.

Historical Cost

Historical costs are real and once established are fixed for the life of the asset or as long as the asset remains on the company's books. For example, when a company purchases a building, the purchase price or historical cost is recorded on the company's balance sheet. However, if that building depreciates in value, the asset is still recorded at the historical cost less depreciation. This accounting practice often results in assets that are carried at significantly off-market prices. Lenders should note that historical costs might overstate or understate asset value.

In a slightly different context, the accounting principle of recording assets at historical cost may lend itself to manipulation as noted in the following trading example. A company with a trading position that is out-the-money (money is lost if the position is closed) may be inclined to roll over that position and either postpone recognizing the loss or hope the market changes and turns the position into a gain.

Accounting Standards as Applied to Revenue Realization

This is one facet of reporting practice to which lenders pay particular attention. Revenues, cash received for merchandise sold or services rendered, are generally recorded at the time of sale or completion of the service. However, two conditions must be met before revenue can be recorded. First, the earnings process must be substantially complete and, second, the collectability of the revenue must be estimated. The earnings process is not substantially complete if:

1. Seller and buyer have not agreed on the price of the merchandise or service.
2. The buyer does not have to pay the seller until the merchandise is resold.
3. The merchandise is stolen or physically destroyed, and the buyer does not have to pay the seller.
4. Intercompany transactions are involved (the buyer and seller are related parties).
5. The seller must continue to provide substantial performance or services to the buyer or aid in reselling the product; if, however, substantial performance has occurred and the collectability of the revenue can be estimated, the sale of the product or service can be recorded.

Revenue recognition, while consistent with applicable accounting standards, may be derived from sources other than operating cash flows. For example, some firms turn retiree-medical plans into a source of profit. Financial Accounting Standard 106, introduced in the early 1990s, required companies to report their total anticipated retiree health care coverage costs. Companies had two incentives to overstate their anticipated costs: (1) excessive costs provided a rational basis to reduce employee benefits; and (2) if the excessive costs proved to be wrong, then the companies could recognize a paper gain by reducing their retiree liability.

The Matching Principle
The popularity of the calendar year as a fiscal period is partly due to the collection of federal income taxes on a calendar-year basis. However, the Internal Revenue Service permits filing tax returns on the basis of a business year instead of a calendar year. GAAP recognizes the concept of matching under the accrual method. The intention is to determine revenue first and then match appropriate costs against revenue. If a financial statement is prepared on another basis of accounting, a statement must be made that the presentation is not in conformity with GAAP. Many small businesses

have chosen this method. By preparing their financial statements on an income tax basis, many of the complexities, such as calculating deferred taxes, are avoided. Thus, the cash method of accounting can be used when preparing a compilation or reviewing a financial statement.

Consistency

While consistency means applying identical methods fiscal year to fiscal year, firms are free to switch from one method of accounting to another, but with restrictions. Firms and their accountants need to demonstrate to lenders and investors that the newly adopted principle is preferable to the old. Then the nature and effect of the accounting change as well as the justification for it must be disclosed in the financial statements for the period in which the change is made.

Disclosure

Sufficient disclosure means more descriptive explanations are provided, including important footnotes. These explanations include detailed disclosure of financial obligations, inventory breakdown, product pricing, and any further disclosure so the audit doesn't become a guessing game. Auditors may add one or more paragraphs to an unqualified report if they feel information is important. This inclusion is known as the emphasis of a matter paragraph and is added before the standard opinion paragraph of an unqualified report.

Objectivity

Lenders want your financial reports to be factual and impartial. While few disclosures are wholly objective, the process must be based on your auditor's sound judgment, diagnostic good sense, and irrefutable background. Reasonable, realistic estimates must be provided, including depreciation charges, deferrals, and accruals of cost, along with revenue items, equity earnings disclosures, restructuring charges, and deferred tax credits. Adequate information is the name of the game and if the figures can be authenticated by independent parties, so much the better. If your lender has doubts, "objectivity" converts to "conservatism." Your accountant should be aware of this. Dr. Howard Schilit suggests that financial statement readers favor firms that present conservative accounting policies[1]:

> Companies that fail to use conservative accounting methods might demonstrate a lack of integrity in their financial reporting process. Indeed, many analysts place a premium on companies that use conservative accounting policies. In searching for excellent companies, for example, the widely respected analyst and shenanigan buster Thornton O'Glove offers the following advice: Look for companies that use very conservative accounting principles. In my experience, if a company does not cut corners in its accounting, there's a good chance it doesn't cut corners in its operations. You know you've got your money with a high quality management.

THE SIGNIFICANCE OF FOOTNOTES

Smart lenders read annual reports cover-to-cover, paying heed to small-print items. After all, there is more to a financial report than just numbers. We find the chairman's optimistic statement, a historical record of 3 or more years, pictures of smiling employees, the latest hot products, charts Andy Wahol would proudly remake into museum-quality prints, and wonderfully vivid graphs. Of course, there are the footnotes, where real information is to be found.

Footnotes are integral to financial statements but are often overlooked because they tend to be technical and frequently appear in small print. Footnotes are the accountant's way of disclosing details of crucial data such as accounting policies and procedures, forthcoming litigation, long-term purchase commitments, changes in accounting principles or estimates, industry-related notes, and segment information.

As an integral part of financial reports, a statement identifies accounting policies adopted and followed by the reporting entity. The APB believes disclosure should be given in a separate summary of significant accounting policies preceding the notes to the financial statements or

---

[1] Schilit H, Perler J. Financial shenanigans: how to detect accounting gimmicks & fraud in financial reports. 3rd ed. McGraw-Hill; April 14, 2010.

Howard Schilit, PhD, CPA, is the founder and CEO of Schilit Forensics, LLC. Dr. Schilit is a pioneer in the field of detecting accounting tricks in corporate financial reports that mislead investors. He has been a leading spokesman before the US Congress, the SEC, and global media outlets about the causes and early warning signs of accounting tricks in public filings.

as the initial note. After reviewing the disclosure of accounting policies, lenders will generally seek information that may negatively impact borrowers, like contingencies. The complete disclosure of material contingencies is an important property of financial statements, according to International Accounting Standards guidelines, because of the uncertainties that may exist at the conclusion of each accounting period.[2]

ACCOUNTING FOR CONTINGENCIES

Standards governing accounting for loss contingencies require accrual and/or note disclosure when specified recognition and disclosure criteria are met. Gain contingencies generally are not recognized in financial statements but can be disclosed. Auditing criteria recognize the high probability that estimate changes will occur in the near term. Below are examples of the types of situations that may require disclosure in accordance with SOP 94-6:

1. Specialized equipment subject to technological obsolescence
2. Valuation allowances for deferred tax assets based on future taxable income
3. Capitalized motion picture film production costs
4. Inventory subject to rapid technological obsolescence
5. Capitalized computer software costs
6. Deferred policy acquisition costs of insurance enterprises
7. Valuation allowances for commercial and real estate loans
8. Environmental remediation-related obligations
9. Litigation-related obligations
10. Contingent liabilities for obligations of other entities
11. Amounts reported for long-term obligations like pensions
12. Expected loss on disposition of a business or assets
13. Amounts reported for long-term contracts

Classification of Contingencies
1. Probable: likely to materialize
2. Reasonably possible: halfway between probable and remote
3. Remote: slight chance of materializing

---

[2] Financial Accounting Standards Board Statement No. 5, Accounting for Contingencies.

Lenders are particularly watchful of general loss contingencies. General loss contingencies may arise from risk of exposure to the following:

1. Product warranties or defects
2. Pending or threatened litigation
3. Risk of catastrophe, that is, losses
4. Direct guarantees – guarantor makes payment to creditor if debtor fails to do so
5. Claims and assessments
6. Pre-acquisition contingencies

Product Warranties or Defects

A warranty (product guarantee) is a promise – for a specific time period – made by a seller to a buyer to make good on a deficiency of quantity, quality, or performance in a product. Warranties can result in future cash outlays, frequently significant additional outlays. Although the future cost is indefinite with regard to amount, due date, and even customer, a liability – an estimate of costs incurred after sale and delivery associated with defect correction – does exist and experienced lenders ask accountants or management to quantify the downside effect.

Litigation Contingencies

Publicly traded companies are required to disclose litigation contingencies when eventual loss from a lawsuit is possible. Studies were done on the classification of predisposition years (years before the year of court adjudication or settlement). It was found that 47.6% of surveyed companies showed unsatisfactory disclosure with no mention of the litigation in financial statements, or a strong disclaimer of liability did not accompany mention of the litigation. Legal action includes antitrust, patent infringement, fraud or misrepresentation, breach of contract, and other noninsurable suits.

The survey above represents a banker's bona fide red flag, if ever there was one. Contingencies such as product lawsuit losses can show up from nowhere, are often explosive, and can finish off an otherwise profitable company in the process. The best hedge against litigation contingencies is preparation, which often means a present value analysis. This means placing values on material lawsuits by determining present value. Minor lawsuits, on the other hand, are usually irrelevant; a court's adverse opinion will not impact equity, debt service, or the borrower's sustainable cash flows.

On the other hand, if we consider General Motors, can litigation be settled? If so, when and for how much? Other questions are following:

- If litigation cannot be settled, when will the court hear the case?
- What are the probabilities the court will render an adverse opinion?
- If the opinion is adverse, will there be grounds for appeal?
- If so, when will the appeal be heard?
- What are the probabilities the appeal will collapse?
- Given the time value of money and the joint probabilities of adverse opinions including appeals, what is the expected present value of the product lawsuit (use face amounts, not expected reduced awards)?
- Pro forma expected losses on fiscal spreadsheets. Is the financial structure strong enough to absorb expected losses?
- Related to the above questions, how do adjusted (pro forma) debt and cash-flow coverage ratios stack against the industry or benchmarks? Has the borrower's industry quartile ranking deteriorated? What is the anticipated impact on bond ratings and/or the bank's credit grade?

Environmental Contingencies

Environmental protection laws pose many dangers for unwary lenders. To avoid potentially unlimited liability that may result from environmental violations, prudent lenders try to extract out expected present values and adjust financials accordingly. Environmental trouble spots include, but are not restricted to:

- Transportation of hazardous substances
- Real property
- The disposition of hazardous substances
- Manufacturing processes that involve use, creation, or disposition of hazardous wastes
- Petroleum or chemicals stored on the premises
- Underground storage tanks
- Equipment used to transport hazardous materials
- Pipes leading to waterways

Risk of Catastrophic Losses

It might be a good idea if lenders worried more about the possibility that some borrowers may face the risk of catastrophic loss. Two criteria must be met to classify a gain or loss as an extraordinary item:

- *Unusual:* The event is one that is unrelated to the typical activities of the business.
- *Nonrecurring:* The event is one that management does not expect to occur again.

Natural disasters meet the definition of unusual (unrelated to the typical activities of the business). For example, a corn farmer in Kansas hit by a drought would not classify the loss as nonrecurring and thus the loss could not be considered extraordinary. On the other hand, a flood in Phoenix would give rise to an extraordinary loss. The criteria "unusual" and "nonrecurring" must be considered from the standpoint of the firm's geographical location and business.

Direct and Indirect Guarantees

Direct guarantees, representing a direct connection between creditor and guarantor, warrant that the guarantor will make payment to the creditor if the debtor fails to do so. In an indirect guarantee, the guarantor agrees to transfer funds to the debtor if a specified event occurs. Indirect guarantees connect the guarantor to the debtor directly, but benefit the creditor indirectly.

FASB 5 requires that the nature and amount of the guarantee be disclosed in financial statements. Guarantees to repurchase receivables or related property, obligations of banks under letters of credit or standby agreements, guarantees of the indebtedness of others, and unconditional obligations to make payments are examples of the types of guarantee contingencies that must be disclosed even if they have a remote possibility of materializing.

FINANCIAL INSTRUMENTS WITH OFF BALANCE SHEET RISK

While corporate executives claim off balance sheet financing instruments are used to mitigate risks, these instruments can function as speculative tools. Borrowers experiencing difficulty may use instruments to improve results not attainable through normal operating activities.

The market crash of 1987 suddenly revealed some large sophisticated companies that had taken inordinately large (that is, beyond the size required for risk management) derivative positions that resulted in significant losses. Under extraordinary circumstances these derivative positions can weaken a credit. Lenders find out about these positions. Here are some examples:

1. A recourse obligation on receivables or bills receivables sold
2. Interest rate and currency swaps, caps and floors
3. Loan commitments and options written on securities; futures contracts
4. Obligations arising from financial instruments sold short
5. Synthetic asset swap which might result in an unwind if the bond goes into default
6. Obligations to repurchase securities sold

Asset Securitization

If an asset can generate cash flow, it can be securitized. When a company securitizes its assets, those assets are sold as a "true sale" and are no longer assets of the company. In fact, many times that is precisely the reason why companies securitize assets: to get them off their balance sheets to improve their profitability ratios. However, some have argued that securitization may inadvertently cause adverse selection for the company's remaining assets; when the company securitizes its best assets (the assets most marketable and easiest to securitize) and retains its poorer assets, the action causes an adverse selection.

Creditors face little risk in the event of bankruptcy because assets can be quickly liquidated. In exchange, however, the creditor receives a lower return on its investments. In addition, if these creditors liquidate the securitized assets, the company will be further unable to recover from a financial crisis and will put its general creditors at even greater risk. Other risks beside credit default include maturity mismatch and prepayment volatility. As a side note, lenders and investors can reduce contingency risks by using computer software containing models and structural and analytical data for asset securitizations, including commercial loan securitizations, and whole-loan and senior-subordinated securities, as well as home equity loans.

Futures Contracts

A commodity such as copper used for production may be purchased for current delivery or for future delivery. Investing in commodity futures refers to the buying or the selling of a contract to deliver a commodity in the future. In the case of a purchase contract, the buyer agrees to accept a specific commodity that meets a specified quality in a specified month. In the case of a sale, the seller agrees to deliver the specified commodity during the designated month. Hedging against unexpected increases in raw material costs is a wise move; speculating in commodity futures, with the bank's money, is another story. There is a large probability that the firm will suffer a loss on any particular purchase or sale of a commodity contract.

Management may purchase a contract for future delivery. This is known as a long position, in which the firm will profit if the price of the commodity, say copper, rises. Management may also enter into a contract for future delivery (short position). These long and short positions run parallel to the long and short positions in security markets.

Pensions

Pension expense represents the amount of money that management should invest at the end of the year to cover future pension payments that will be made to employees for this additional year's service. Accounting records reflect management's best guess as to real pension costs. Accountants try to measure the cost of these retirement benefits at the time the employee earns them, rather than when the employee actually receives them. A multiplicity of pension assumptions needs to be compiled to come up with the required pension amount. These include the following:

- Interest invested funds are expected to earn
- Number of years an employee is expected to live after retirement
- Salary of employee at retirement
- Average years of service of an employee at retirement

Beware of unfunded projected benefit obligations since this liability indicates that pension investments fall short of future pension benefits. Borrowers that continuously fund less than current pension expense, or that incorporate unrealistic assumptions in their pension plans could find themselves embedded in a thicket of thorns in the not-too-distant future.

Companies with defined benefit pension plans must disclose three items: (1) pension discount rate, (2) expected rate of future compensation increases, and (3) projected long-term rate of return on pension assets. Understanding what these figures mean provides insight into, for example, whether a merger candidate's pension liabilities make it worth less than meets the eye, and how companies use perfectly legal (but fairly sneaky) accounting gimmicks to inflate profits.

Discretionary Items

Some expenditures are discretionary, meaning they fall under management's control, including the following:

- Repair and maintenance of equipment
- Research and development
- Marketing and advertising expenditures
- New product lines, acquisitions and divestitures of operating units

Management might forgo timely equipment repairs in order to improve earnings, but the policy could backfire over the longer term.

Research and Development

In its Statement of Financial Accounting Standards No. 2, "Accounting for Research and Development Costs" (October 1974), the Financial Accounting Standards Board concludes, "All research and development costs encompassed by this Statement shall be charged to expense when incurred." The FASB (Statement No. 2) and the SEC (ASR No. 178) mandated all companies to expense R&D outlays. The Board reached its conclusion as a result of a reasoning process in which several preliminary premises were accepted as true.

- Uncertainty of future benefits: R&D expenditures often are undertaken even when there is a small probability of success. The Accounting Board mentioned that the high degree of uncertainty of realizing the future benefits of individual research and development projects was a significant factor in reaching this conclusion.
- Lack of causal relationship between expenditures and benefits
- R&D does not meet the accounting concept of an asset
- Matching of revenues and expenses
- Relevance of resulting information for investment and credit decisions.

An incontrovertible solution for avoiding problems dealing with overstating R&D expenditures is to expense costs associated with the acquisition of assets where some significant probability exists that the asset will be worth less than cost. This so-called conservative approach is consistent with guidelines dealing with expensing R&D.

TWO SIGNIFICANT AUDITING STORM SIGNALS

Changing Auditors

When respected auditors are frequently changed, particularly if downtiering occurs, lenders want to know why. Management may cite high auditing fees as the motive for change, but there may also be adverse credit implications foretelling lower-quality disclosures, conflict of interest, and less validation effort. The downtiering in auditors may have been brought on by a difference of opinion between auditor and management regarding treatment and certification of material items. The bank may also check with other lenders sharing the credit or the firm's suppliers. At the very least, the lender will compare the present accountant's certificate with that of the previous auditor to ensure any variances are understood.

Creative Accounting

"Creative accounting" is any method of accounting that overstates revenues or understates expenses. Creative accounting is a sure sign that something is amiss. Lenders view it as a smokescreen to hide real operating results in order to prolong the company's credit standing and to confound investors. It has been a longstanding tradition for borrowers on an economic downspin to pass off inflated financial results, in an attempt to fool lenders into thinking performance was better than it actually was. For example, companies might choose to inflate income, produce fictitious revenues, overstate assets, capitalize expenditures, misappropriate assets, book premature revenues, understate expenses and liabilities, or navigate around accounting rulings governing revenue recognition. Creative accounting shenanigans are a violation of fundamental accounting principles.

CHAPTER 4

Ratios Every Business Should Monitor

OUTLINE

Navigating the Business Loan. http://dx.doi.org/10.1016/B978-0-12-801698-5.00004-2

Veteran lenders can scan your firm's financial statement and know, in a matter of minutes, whether you have hit the can you pay, will you pay bull's-eye. The truth is – lenders do not in fact pore over financial statements until their credit support teams produce ratios. So if you were hoping for a seamless trip through the loan process, be patient. Ratios form the structure of fundamental analysis, and establish the basis of preliminary loan discussions, so prudent lenders will likely defer further discussion until they have had a chance to review your firm's ratios. Before you meet with your lender, learn what ratios are all about, what they say about your business, and how to make them work in your favor.

WHAT ARE RATIOS?

A ratio compares values and reveals how much of one measure there is with respect to another measure. If you tell your lender the firm made $2 million profits last year, do not be disappointed if your lender is unimpressed. The value – $2 million – is in fact an absolute number floating in space. However, $2 million profits on $10 million sales means every dollar in sales produced two cents profits, a relative measure of performance that means something. Ratios simplify absolute numbers by converting numbers to a common scale. However, useful as they are, ratios cannot tell the full story.

Ratios offer clues, not direct answers. It would be unreasonable for you to think that the mechanical calculation of one ratio or a group of ratios automatically yields factual information about your business. Only you can evaluate past performance, assess the firm's present position, and obtain a relative value to compare with competition. Does your company earn a fair return? Can it withstand downturns? Does it have the financial flexibility to qualify for low-cost loans or attract additional investors? Is your management team adroit in its efforts to upgrade slow operations, reinforce strong ones, pursue profitable opportunities, and push value to the highest possible levels?

Ratios are indeed imperfect, so plan your response ahead of time. If your lender views specific ratios as lackluster, you should be able to retort with a convincing counter-augment. For example, time-series and cross-sectional analysis may be distorted by inflation or an unusual business climate. The trick is to determine the nature of bias and follow through with adjustments to make ratios meaningful. In addition, because financial statements are routinely prepared for special purposes, such as reports to shareholders and creditors, financials may be more liberal than realistic.

Undeniably, the application of ratio analysis necessitates benchmark comparisons (performance of your business against others) if information is to be meaningful. Here are a few considerations as we begin to think about ratios:

1. Our ratios apply to manufacturers, wholesalers, retailers, and service companies. We employ different ratio sets to analyze banks, utilities, insurance, and finance companies. Divergent asset quality and capital structure make it necessary to employ other ratios.
2. Ratios concentrate on the past; loan repayment is a future event.
3. Borrowers may window-dress financial statements to make them look better.
4. Benchmarks or industry leaders are better targets for high-level performance. Bankers tend to match customers against solid performers; average performance may not be good enough.
5. Data quality and availability could diminish ratio utility.

Peer Group or Industry Comparisons

Comparative ratio analysis is highly informative. Under certain circumstances, lenders might question the validity of comparative ratios, especially when they compare ratios to industry norms without knowing a borrower's history. In addition, keep in mind the performances of the rest of the industry and suitable industrial averages against which your firm is benchmarked. You may begin to question ratio comparisons when your business cycle differs from that of the rest of the industry. This difference may create an illusion of poor or exaggerated ratios (in terms of performance) when in fact nothing could be further from the truth. For example, firms displaying high current or quick ratios may be viewed as liquid, meaning they can convert current assets into cash quickly and meet expenses, when in reality high current ratios may be the result of inefficient resource utilization.

We might find it difficult to compare a diversified firm's financial statement to industry averages. We are not really comparing like numbers; the firm's ratios may be composed of figures tied to numerous industries and varied operations. Smart bankers do not jump to conclusions about ratio quality, magnitude, and trend. Instead, they evaluate companies on their own merits, continuously asking if ratios are composed of the right stuff. A comparison of Large Firm, Inc. with Miniature Firm, Inc., for example, would not easily yield accurate comparative information. Large Firm is a big operation with financial statements different from Small Firm, though both firms are in the same industry. Or consider the case of General Dynamics Electric Boat. Electric Boat has a few very expensive submarines listed on its balance sheet and if management disposed of one submarine just before or after the end of a fiscal period, that action could greatly influence comparisons.

Assets themselves can lead to different levels of ratio quality. Samsung's reputation is built on smartphones, tablets, and televisions. However, Samsung's business activities are spread far beyond consumer markets. The electronics giant also makes military hardware, apartments, and ships, and operates a Korean amusement park! Imagine how difficult it would be if you were asked to compare Samsung's consolidated current ratio to a competitor's. Walmart's foray into groceries, Indigo's expansion into giftware, Olay's move from wrinkle creams to beauty products, and banks adding insurance services and wealth management to their portfolios are all examples of how it is nearly impossible to ascertain the extent to which differing product lines contribute to the bottom lines of two firms being ratio compared. Notably, consolidating financial statements (vs. consolidated financials) are superior instruments for uncovering performance detail.

In the highly volatile capital markets industry, we might find it hard to establish a meaningful set of comparative industry averages. The various methods of classifying assets and liabilities in this business combined with market volatility result in a comparison quandary. Companies specializing in niche markets that cater to specialized markets pose still another problem. The Concorde Jet, for example, was the sole entity in its market, with no other firms against which its performance could be compared.

Companies vary in size within an industry, which might distort ratios, and some firms may straddle more than one industry. Some industries, such as biotechnology, are volatile. Similarly, each firm has diverse contingencies such as patents, litigation, licensing agreements, and joint ventures, affecting comparisons. Additional problems arise with the use of industry averages. Norms only represent the center, and therefore, the actual position of the company within its peer group often is not clear. For example, Walmart has an outsized effect on its industry. Material size differences might make it difficult to canvass industries and pick the right benchmarks. Large firms tend to operate efficiently because of economies of scale and high operating leverage. For example, Sears functions more efficiently than small retail establishments. Ratio comparisons might be inaccurate since Sears has a good-sized bearing on the benchmark.

Geographic differences can also affect companies in the same industry. For example, how does a banker compare ratios of two home-building companies and come up with the right answer? It is not easy. One firm may do business on the East Coast while the other may operate in California. Both firms are grouped in one broad industry classification – regional home builders. Because of differences in local economies, cultures, and demographics, ratios of the two home builders are bound to be heterogeneous.

Another problem surfaces when lenders attempt to analyze a youthful firm or industry. New businesses lack history, making it difficult to track historical trends and predict future performance. Three-dimensional printing and remote manufacturing create solid structures from digital computer files; if objects can be printed remotely in the home or office, it will potentially revolutionize the economics of manufacturing.

Energy-efficient water purification offers the potential for significantly higher energy efficiency in desalination or purification of wastewater, potentially reducing energy consumption by 50% or more. Further examples include carbon dioxide conversion and use, remote sensing, and precise drug delivery through nanoscale engineering. Another industry that comes to mind from the not-so-distant past is the software industry. It was not long ago that this industry was small and developing. The space industry, with its associated research and development firms, further illustrates the difficulty in establishing meaningful benchmark comparisons.

Different accounting practices sometimes distort ratio comparisons as well: FIFO versus LIFO, leasing versus financing, accounts receivable provisions, capitalized expenses, differing depreciation methods, and research and development costs accounting can all distort ratio comparisons. Since comparative financial ratios are based on accounting numbers, the possibility of dissimilar firms or even diverse divisions within a company employing distinctive accounting can lead any analyst down the wrong path. Sometimes ratios do not reflect ongoing operations, which might confound lenders when they compare net margins to industry averages. Also, some firms use different year-ends, and this practice may alter financials and distort comparisons.

Another difficulty lies in comparing international firms or foreign-owned companies. The influence of government regulation on these entities must be considered as well. How do foreign-owned companies' accounting methods differ from U.S. practice? International accounting has recently become standardized, thankfully. International Financial Reporting Standards, or IFRS, refers to a set of international accounting standards that define how different types of transactions and other accounting events should be reported in financial statements. International companies frequently have complex accounting needs, as they must substantiate balances for multiple accounting standards around the globe, such as U.S. GAAP and IFRS or local statutory standards and IFRS.

One area of benchmark comparisons in which ratio analysis is simply insufficient is seasonal businesses. Because the flows and contractions of these companies do not always coincide, lenders usually find it challenging to peg an industry average. This will, of course, depend on whether credit departments calculate ratios prior to or after seasonal peaks.

Indeed, it is essential to decipher ratios using good judgment. For example, good sense suggests that Ghana bankers seek local benchmarks initially, not (ratio) downloads from the sources from the United States or the United Kingdom (the proverbial apples and oranges). When creditors work with ratio comparatives, they usually rank two comparisons, the company to an industry and the industry to another industry. There may be unique qualities that cause valid differences in the comparison, meaning the creditor should have at least as much industry knowledge as the borrower does in order to select appropriate benchmarks. Industry averages should be avoided in favor of specific benchmarks, such as local businesses. If your lender is conformable with averages, he or she should at least check to see if your firm's ratios exceed one standard deviation from the median.

Ratio comparatives serve as guides, and only guides. Come back with a good sell if your lender informs you that results were disappointing compared to competitors. At the very least, bankers should communicate with knowledgeable individuals – accountants, consultants, suppliers or internal industry specialists – before bringing ratio comparatives to the table.

Ratio Trends

Are financial trends consistent with the past, or do ratios reveal troublesome departures from historical trends? Lenders have likely experienced more disappointments than they would care to admit – that is, deals in which loans went bad because nobody picked up on unexpected trends. Here is one example: a seasonal amusement park operator, historically cash rich during the tourist season, needed to borrow off-season to pay expenses. Interim statements depicted the usual seasonal expansion and contraction processes. A newly assigned relationship manager noticed that the obligor's loan was fully extended during mid-August and began asking questions. The outcome: the borrower diverted cash normally used to repay the bank loan into a new fledgling enterprise, and could not repay the credit line.

Ratio Workshop

It is time to dig in. Financial ratios separate into explicit groupings: liquidity ratios, activity or performance ratios, leverage or capital structure ratios, profitability ratios, and growth and valuation ratios. Valuation ratios will be reviewed in Chapter 9. The ensuing short case of Jones Designs, Inc. centers on ratio calculations and discussion of individual ratios.

Jones Designs, Inc.

The loan officer at First Central Bank was recently alerted to the deteriorating financial position of the bank's client, Jones Designs, Inc. If any ratio falls significantly below industry averages provided, computers flag deficiencies and produce exception reports. Loan terms require that certain ratios be maintained at specified minimum levels. When an analysis was run on Jones Designs 3 months ago, the firm's banker noticed that key ratios continued to trend down, falling below industry averages. The banker sent a copy of the computer output to management along with a note voicing concern.

Initial analysis indicated that problems were developing, but no ratio was below the level specified in the loan agreement between bank and borrower. However, the second analysis, which was based on the data given in Table 4.1, showed that the current ratio was below the 2.0 times specified in the loan agreement.

Table 4.1 Jones Designs, Inc. Ratio Trends				
Ratio	*2012*	*2013*	*2014*	**Industry**
Current ratio	3.05	2.67	1.75	2.50
Quick ratio	1.65	1.08	0.73	1.00
Average collection period	37 days	37 days	55 days	32 days
Inventory turnover	7.1×	4.5×	3.6×	5.7×
Fixed asset turnover	11.7×	12.0×	12.1×	12.1×
Working capital turnover	6.2×	5.3×	5.6×	4.5×
Total asset turnover	3.0×	2.5×	2.0×	2.8×
Average settlement period	18 days	26 days	44 days	35 days
Gross profit margin	19.9%	17.7%	13.8%	18.0%
Selling, general, and administration expenses	8.7%	10.2%	13.8%	9.3%
Net profit margin	5.5%	3.4%	0.39%	2.90%
Return on total assets	16.8%	8.9%	0.7%	8.8%
Return on net worth	28.3%	16.7%	2.0%	17.5%
Dividend payout rate	25.3%	23.8%	13.5%	7%
Debt ratio (debt/assets)	40.6%	46.5%	59.87%	50.0%
Times interest earned	15.8×	7.9×	1.4×	7.7×

The loan agreement specified that the bank could call for immediate payment of the entire bank loan, and if payment was not forthcoming within 10 days, the bank could call the loan, forcing Jones Designs, Inc. into bankruptcy. The banker had no intention of actually enforcing loan covenants at this time, but instead intended to use the loan agreement to encourage management to take decisive action to improve the firm's financial condition.

Jones Designs manufactures a line of costume jewelry. In addition to creating its regular merchandise, Trudy creates special items for the holiday season. Seasonal working capital requirements are financed by a $300,000 line of credit. In accordance with standard banking practices, however, the loan agreement requires repayment in full at some time during the year, in this case by February 2014. Higher raw material costs, together with increased wages, led to a decline in the firm's profit margin during the last half of 2013, as well as during most of 2014. Sales increased during both of these years, thanks to the firm's aggressive marketing program, despite competition from shell and turquoise jewelry makers.

The company received a copy of the banker's ratio analysis along with a letter informing management that the bank would insist on immediate repayment of the entire loan unless the firm submitted a business plan showing how operations could be turned around. Management felt that sales levels could not improve without an increase in the bank loan from $300,000 to $400,000, since payments of $100,000 for construction of a plant addition would have to be made in January 2015. While the firm had been the bank's loyal customer for over 50 years, management questioned whether the bank would continue to supply the present line of credit, let alone approve facility increases.

The banker examined exigent ratios with the client, centering on strengths and weaknesses revealed by the ratio analysis. He wanted to know specifically the amount of internal funds that could have been available for debt payment if fiscal performance were at industry levels, with particular focus on the two working capital accounts, receivables and inventory. After meeting with management, the bank reviewed alternatives and arrived at a credit decision. Fiscal statements follow:

Jones Designs, Inc.
Balance Sheet
Year Ended December 31
($ Thousands)

Assets		2012	2013	2014
1.	Current Assets			
2.	Cash and cash items	15,445	12,007	11,717
3.	Accounts and notes receivable, net	51,793	55,886	88,571
4.	Inventories	56,801	99,087	139,976
5.	**Current Assets**	**124,039**	**166,980**	**240,264**
6.	Property, plant, & equipment	53,282	60,301	68,621
7.	Accumulated Depreciation	(8,989)	(13,961)	(20,081)
8.	**Net Fixed Assets**	**44,294**	**46,340**	**48,539**
9.	**Total Assets**	**168,333**	**213,320**	**288,803**
Liabilities and Equities		**2012**	**2013**	**2014**
10.	**Current Liabilities**			
11.	Short-term loans	10,062	15,800	55,198
12.	Accounts payable	20,292	31,518	59,995
13.	Accruals	10,328	15,300	21,994
14.	**Current Liabilities**	**40,682**	**62,618**	**137,187**
15.	Long-term bank loans	19,125	28,688	28,688
16.	Mortgage	8,606	7,803	7,018
17.	**Long Term Debt**	**27,731**	**36,491**	**35,706**
18.	**Total Liabilities**	**68,413**	**99,109**	**172,893**
19.	Common stock (no par value)	69,807	69,807	69,807
20.	Retained Earnings	30,113	44,404	46,103
21.	Stockholders' Equity	99,920	114,211	115,910
22.	**Total Liabilities and Equity**	**168,333**	**213,320**	**288,803**

Jones Designs, Inc.
Income Statement
Year Ended December 31
($ Millions)

		2012	2013	2014
23.	Net Sales	512,693	553,675	586,895
24.	Cost of goods sold	405,803	450,394	499,928
25.	**Gross Profit**	**106,889**	**103,281**	**86,967**
	Cost and expenses:			

		2012	2013	2014
26.	Selling, administration expenses	38,369	46,034	50,643
27.	Depreciation	4,781	4,973	6,120
28.	Miscellaneous expenses	6,082	10,672	17,174
29.	**Total Costs and Expenses**	**49,233**	**61,678**	**73,937**
30.	**Earnings before Interest and Taxes (EBIT)**	**57,658**	**41,602**	**13,030**
	Less interest expense:			
	Interest on ST loans	956	1,683	5,470
	Interest on LT loans	1,913	2,869	2,869
	Interest on mortgage	779	707	636
31.	Total interest expense	3,648	5,258	8,974
32.	**Earnings before Taxes**	**54,010**	**36,343**	**4,056**
33.	Income taxes	26,068	17,589	2,091
34.	**Net Income**	**27,943**	**18,754**	**1,965**
35.	Dividends on stock	7,062	4,463	266
36.	Additions to retained earnings	20,883	14,291	1,699

Liquidity Ratios

Liquidity ratios measure the quality and capability of current assets to meet maturing short-term obligations as they come due. Acceptable liquidity levels depend on economic and industry conditions, the predictability of cash flow, and the quality of assets making up liquidity ratios.

Current Ratio

Defined as current assets/current liabilities, this ratio is a commonly used measure of short-term solvency and debt service. One might surmise that the higher the ratio comparative to industry averages, the better the comfort zone between short-term resources and short-term obligations, but two issues cause this postulation to be incorrect. First, a company blessed with a rapid seasonal conversion cycle usually can get away with a lower current ratio compared to a firm with a sluggish conversion cycle. Secondly, the allocation and quality of key current assets, namely, accounts receivable and inventory, is of great importance in determining acceptable ratio levels. The company's current ratio at year-end 2014 is shown below.

Current Assets:	
Cash	11,717
Accounts receivable	88,571
Inventories	*139,976*
Current assets	240,264
Current liabilities:	
Short-term loans	55,198
Accounts payable	59,995
Accruals	21,994
Current liabilities	137,187

Current ratio = current assets over current liabilities = $240,264/$137,187 = 1.75

2012	2013	2014	Industry Average
3.05	2.67	1.75	2.50

The borrower's current ratio declined over the past 3 years, falling below the industry average. An accounts receivable buildup points to worsening aging, in addition to increased possibilities of bad debt write-offs. Furthermore, inventory has increased. Although some financial writers maintain that "high is best" magnitude means little if receivable and inventory quality fall below acceptable levels.

Quick Ratio (Also Known As Acid Test)
The quick ratio is a more conservative measure of liquidity because it measures a firm's ability to pay off all short-term obligations without relying on the sale of inventory. Since the quick ratio isolates the most liquid assets, it is more accurate than the current ratio. This can be of particular importance if inventory consists of a large portion of current assets.

Quick ratio = cash and accounts receivable/current liabilities = $11,717 + $88,571/$137,187 = 0.73

2012	2013	2014	Industry Average
1.65	1.08	0.73	1.00

During the past 3 years, we notice that Jones Designs's quick ratio eroded, dropping below the industry average. In most cases, if the quick ratio is below one, borrowers can't pay off current liabilities without selling inventory. At a time when financial performance is deteriorating, the firm may be forced to sell inventory at below cost to pay existing obligations.

Net Working Capital
Returning to the current ratio for one moment, closer inspection shows that this ratio is another way to reveal net working capital position. Net working capital – current assets minus current liabilities – measures the amount of money left over if current assets liquidate at face value.

Net working capital = current assets − current liabilities = \$240,264 − \$137,187 = \$103,077

Activity or Turnover Ratios
Receivable turnover and inventory turnover, two important activity or asset turnover ratios, correlate to sales, the outcome of which determines how efficiently management utilizes resources it commands with respect to sales. Lenders pay close attention to these two ratios because success depends on both solid customer portfolios and inventory that moves. We review the average collection period (same results as accounts receivable turnover), inventory turnover, fixed asset turnover, total asset turnover, and working capital turnover.

Average Collection Period
The average collection period (ACP) determines the time it takes to convert accounts receivable into cash. ACP factors can be external or internal. For example, economic fluctuations affecting a specific business sector will affect the number of days until payments arrive. If only a few companies are affected, lenders tend to blame the firm's management, not the industry.

Average collection period = (accounts receivables/sales) × 365 = \$88,571/\$586,895 × 365 = 55 days

2012	2013	2014	Industry average
37	37	55	32 days

A tight ACP usually suggests high-quality receivables and improved cash flow. Conversely, increases over the past 3 years may mean cash flow problems, which might lead lenders to request an accounts receivable aging schedule. An aging schedule quickly points to collection difficulties that may result in lost revenues and higher bad debt expenses. Weak collection periods hint at stale inventory and a host of other financial woes. However, there is another side to this coin. Increases may mean liberal credit standards aimed at attracting new customers, increasing market share, and making more money.

First Central Bank should first rule out macroeconomic and industry forces since these two forces are exogenous. For instance, if management argues receivables slowed up due to a sluggish economy, bankers will compare that finding to benchmarks or industry average. However, the industry average is 32, not 54 days. Perhaps 22 days' difference does not sound like much but if cash flow is compromised, watch out!

How worrisome are small shifts in the average collection period? Let us replace the firm's 54-day average collection period with the 32-day industry average, and enter the firm's fiscal sales (365 is a constant). We solve for a new dependent variable – pro forma accounts receivable – that is, fiscal 2014 receivables the firm would have posted on its balance sheet had management been as collection-efficient as the industry average. Here is the result:

Recall that the average collection period = (accounts receivables/ sales) $\times$ 365 = \$88,571/\$586,895 $\times$ 365 = 55

Now solve for pro forma 2014 fiscal accounts receivable given 2014 fiscal sales \$586,895 and industry average collection period of 32 days.

Thus, 2014 accounts receivable pro forma = 32 (\$586,895)/365 = \$52,905

Fiscal receivables minus pro forma receivables = \$88,571 – \$52,905 = \$35,667, indicating at fiscal date good money was floating in space (in the possession of customers). In other words, fiscal cash flow had been compromised to the tune of \$35,667 simply because receivables were not paid. Smart lenders employing similar pro forma techniques can differentiate between accounts receivable increases linked to normal growth as opposed to receivable increases tied to lackluster collection efforts. In this example, Jones Designs, Inc.'s lenders will ask for supplemental information – receivable aging, customer list, collection efforts, credit standards, credit terms, and trade discounts, since it is possible the firm has exchanged one weak asset – stale inventory – for another, lower quality receivables.

Bad Debt Expense/Sales
Lenders evaluate receivables quality making use of the ratio bad debt expense/sales. A higher bad-debt-to-sales ratio usually indicates lax credit standards or compromised financial condition of the customer.

Inventory Turnover
The inventory turnover depicts the number of times inventory turned over during a fiscal year and is usually benchmarked to industry results. Inventory control is crucial to well-run operations, and depends on the interrelationship between raw materials, work-in-process, and finished goods. Raw material inventory relates to your firm's anticipated production, seasonality, and reliability of suppliers. If raw material inventories are salable and commodity-like, your lender will view inventory as more liquid than, say, work-in-process inventory. While raw materials may be more liquid, a large amount of raw materials on hand may also indicate speculative holdings in anticipation of price increases or shortages. Work-in-process inventory is associated with the length of the production cycle. Dynamics include manufacturing efficiency, product engineering techniques, and maintenance of skilled workers. Excessive work-in-process inventory suggests production slowdowns and/or manufacturing inefficiencies, which could turn into a nightmare scenario if you have to inform customers that shipments will be delayed.

A high turnover ratio is not automatically good. Stock-outs, which lead to lost sales, may be due to the incapacity to accurately project sales patterns or master production. The clues are all there, concealed within the ratio.

Inventory turnover (cost) = cost of goods sold/inventory = $499,928/$139,976 = 3.6

Inventory turnover (sales) = sales/inventory = $586,895/ $139,976 = 4.2

2012	2013	2014	Industry Average
7.1	4.5	3.6	5.7
9.0	5.6	4.2	7.0

In the case of Jones Designs, inventory turnover fell below the industry average and is trending downward, suggesting (1) too much inventory on hand, (2) liquidity may be worse than indicated (by the current ratio), and (3) inventory could be obsolete and may need to be written off.

The Fixed Asset Turnover

Directing the firm's capital equipment policies is central to management's goal of maximizing shareholder value. Investment in fixed assets reduces cash flow in periods when investments are made. As a result, cash generated by productive assets must offset initial investment outflows, producing a positive net present value. In other words, this ratio reflects cash flow quality and sustainability.

Fixed asset turnover = sales/net fixed assets = \$586,895/\$48,539 = 12.09

2012	2013	2014	Industry Average
11.7	12.0	12.1	12.1

Jones Designs, Inc.'s fixed asset turnover is in level with the industry's fixed asset turnover. Let us review the cues suggesting that the firm is operating fixed assets efficiently. A high ratio suggests the following:

1. The firm's efficient use of property plant and equipment has resulted in a high level of operating capacity.
2. Merger and divestment activity has changed the composition and size of fixed assets on the consolidated balance sheet.
3. The firm has increased plant capacity, utilizing more machines.
4. Old equipment was sold.

There is a negative side to this ratio. For example, a high turnover ratio may indicate that management allowed plant facilities to wear down. The big question that remains is whether high turnover is good or bad. Your lender will examine the fiscal cash flow seeking answers (Chapter 6). The following are a few warning signals the lender will watch for:

• The cash flow statement reveals a deferred tax runoff.
• Depreciation expense (related to older machinery) is larger than capital expenditures (related to replacement costs).
• Unfilled orders (backlogs) increase.
• Work-in-process inventory expands due to production slowdowns.

- Reduced operating leverage as additional labor is channeled to production.
- Gross profit margin eroded appreciably.

Working Capital Turnover

Working capital is a general measure of liquidity and represents the margin of protection short-term creditors expect. As we saw earlier, working capital is the excess of current assets over current liabilities. Sufficient working capital is essential to meet operating needs along with supplier and short-term debt obligations.

Working capital turnover = sales/working capital = $586,895/ $103,077 = 5.6

2012	2013	2014	Industry Average
6.2	5.3	5.6	4.5

Total Asset Turnover

How efficiently does a firm utilize capital? How many sales dollars are generated by each total asset dollar?

Total asset turnover = sales/total assets = $586,895/$288,803 = 2.0

2012	2013	2014	Industry Average
3.0	2.5	2.0	2.8

In 2014 total asset turnover dipped significantly below the industry average, suggesting that the firm had to employ more assets per sales dollar than the industry average, implying reduced asset productivity. By the process of elimination, since the fixed assets turnover is equal to the industry's, problems in this business can be traced to receivables and inventory (current asset management).

Average Settlement Period or Accounts Payable Turnover

The average settlement period measures the time it takes to pay creditors. The accounts payable turnover is the number of times trade payables turn over in 1 year.

Average settlement period = accounts payable/average purchases per day

Accounts payable turnover = cost of goods sold/accounts payable

Average settlement period = (accounts payable/cost of goods sold) ×
365 = \$59,995/\$499,928 × 365 = 44 days

2012	2013	2014	Industry Average
18	26	44	35

High ratios suggest shorter time between purchase and payment. If,
for example, the firm's payables turned over slower than benchmark's,
likely causes would include disputed invoices, extended terms, late payments, and cash flow problems.

Profitability Ratios

Management's success at production and expense control, as well as its
ability to counter economic and industry downturns, plus a number of
hybrid factors contribute to this mainstream ratio group.

The Gross Profit Margin

The gross profit margin measures production success and is an integral
part of the lending toolbox because it is especially adept at differentiat-
ing between temporary and structural problems. Were higher production costs successfully passed to consumers? Are raw materials costs adequately controlled? Is the labor/machine mix optimal? Do production
policies and methods measure favorably against benchmark firms? What
is the degree of operating leverage? Operating leverage is an important
constituent of this ratio. For example, to a physicist, leverage means
raising a heavy object with a small force using a lever. In business, a high
degree of operating leverage means that relatively small changes in sales
result in large changes in operating income.

Gross profit = net sales − cost of goods sold (net sales = gross sales
− returns, allowances, discounts)

Cost of goods sold = beginning inventory + purchases + overhead
+ factory labor + factory depreciation + freight in − ending inventory

Gross profit margin = gross profit/net sales = \$86,967/\$586,895
= 14.8%

2012	2013	2014	Industry Average
19.9%	17.7%	13.8%	18.0%

Jones Designs, Inc.'s gross margin has fallen sharply and is significantly below the industry margin. The cause may be the result of a weak pricing policy, high production costs, or a combination of both. Gross profit troubles can usually be traced to poor asset management policies and operating leverage problems, which is likely the case here.

Selling General and Administration Expenses/Sales
This ratio measures management's ability to control costs not associated with production. Expenses higher than historical levels may be justified if they are accompanied by strong product demand. Examples include advertising, promotion, and research expenditures contributing to a strong bottom line.

Selling, general, administration + miscellaneous expenses/net sales = $50,643 + $17,174/$586,895 = 11.5%

2012	2013	2014	Industry Average
8.7%	10.2%	13.8%	9.3%

The ratio of expenses, including miscellaneous expenses, to sales is higher than the industry norm. The firm's accountant included interest cost, meaning this borrower's failure to reduce short-term debt has resulted in higher miscellaneous expenses.

Effective Tax Rate
The provision for income taxes excludes excise, social security, and sales taxes. You may want to compare this rate to the statutory tax rate and to the prior year's effective tax rate.

Effective tax rate = taxes paid/pretax income = $2,091/$4,056 = 51%

2012	2013	2014
48.3%	48.4%	51%

The Net Margin
This important yardstick of success depicts the percentage of each sales dollar remaining after all expenses and taxes have been deducted.

Net margin = net income/net sales = $1,965/$586,895 = 0.34%

2012	2013	2014	Industry Average
5.5%	3.4%	0.39%	2.90%

The firm's low profit margin reflects rising costs and lower increases in revenue. The firm appears to have a production problem evidenced by sharply reduced gross profit margins over 3 years – causes likely to include imbalance between fixed and variable costs, higher raw materials cost, increased overhead, or increased factory labor. High inventory might be responsible for greater storage costs, larger losses from trend changes, and other factors. Operating expenses might also be cut back. Additionally, the low assets turnover shows that the firm has not utilized assets efficiently. If higher sales cannot be produced to bring current assets into line, the firm should consider reducing assets, particularly inventory, which is twice as large as the industry average.

Return on Net Worth

The return on net worth ratio provides the per-dollar yield on investment to the equity holder. The ratio can be expressed as a function of the return on assets, the profit margin, and leverage. If returns are consistently below the risk-free rate of return, why is this business operating?

Return on net worth = net income/average net worth = $1,965/ $115,060 = 1.7%

2012	2013	2014	Industry Average
28.3%	16.7%	2.0%	17.5%

The firm's return to shareholders has fallen significantly and far below the average for the industry.

Return on Total Assets

Also called Return on Investment or ROI, this ratio measures how effectively a company employs its total assets.

Return on total assets = net income/total assets = $1,965/$288,803 = 0.68%

2012	2013	2014	Industry Average
16.8%	8.9%	0.7%	8.8%

While this ratio depicts asset profitability and cost effectiveness, it ignores asset composition, quality, and the debt-to-equity mix. It appears current asset productivity is the primary cause of a continuously deteriorating ratio.

Dividend Payout Ratio

The dividend payout ratio indicates the percentage of earnings paid out in dividends.

Dividend payout ratio = total cash dividends/net income = $266/$1,965 = 13.5%

2012	2013	2014	Industry Average
25.3%	23.8%	13.5%	27%

Lenders may question dividend payout since dividends impact debt-to-equity (leverage). Leverage can easily go out of line if a firm finances generous dividends with large debt increases. Because dividends represent a use of cash (we will see how this works in Chapter 6), creditors target this ratio when debt levels become too high. For example, a historically profitable borrower serving the entertainment industry began paying large dividends financed by bank loans. When the inevitable recession hit, the firm lacked the cash reserves and debt capacity to survive.

Financial Leverage Ratios

This family of ratios depicts the relationship between shareholders' funds and reserves, borrowed funds, and other liabilities. Highly leveraged borrowers, depending on industry values, face greater risk if profits erode. Interest and principal must be repaid, profits or no profits. The big question is: how elevated can leverage be without undermining a borrower's financial structure? The answer depends on a complex set of factors including asset quality, cash flow coverage (of debt service), debt mix (short term vs. long term), sustainable operating and financial factors like revenue growth, and equity market values.

Unlike activity and profitability ratios, financial leverage is not something management necessarily wants to maximize, though asset returns or tax benefits may run higher in highly leveraged firms. Sound strategic plans aim to strike an optimal balance between the benefits of debt and the cost of risk.

Debt-to-Equity and Debt-to-Total Assets Ratios

It is not uncommon for firms with highly liquid assets, like banks, to boast a 9:1 debt-to-equity ratio. On the other hand, manufacturers tend to position leverage below 100%.

Total debt/stockholders equity = debt to equity = $172,893/ $115,910 = 149.1%

Total debt/total assets = debt to total assets

$172,893/$288,803 = 59.9%

2012	2013	2014	Industry Average
40.6%	46.5%	59.87%	50.0%

Debt levels have increased above the industry average. Taken in isolation, this is usually not a concern. However, this borrower's questionable asset quality, together with an apparent imbalance between current and noncurrent liabilities, weak cash flow coverage, and unquestioned low equity value (in real terms) may well have pushed leverage beyond bank tolerance levels.

Take, for example, the case of Bijou Furniture, a borrower that consolidated operations with a competitor to broaden market share. Based on sales projections Bijou was able to finance the acquisition with loans. When sales dropped unexpectedly the firm defaulted on its loans and was forced to sell assets at liquidation value to meet partial payments. The firm's banker might have avoided this headache had he considered the underlying mechanics of leverage ratios in general, and the interdependence of leverage, return, and productivity allied to this acquisition.

Times Interest Earned
This ratio measures how far earnings drop before interest is not covered. The ratio is not as useful as the fixed charge and cash flow coverage ratios.

Times interest earned = earnings before interest and taxes/interest = $13,030/$8,973 = 1.4

2012	2013	2014	Industry Average
15.8	7.9	1.4	7.7

The firm covers interest costs with only 1.4× earnings. It appears that profits will not be available to make much of a dent in paying down principal.

The Fixed Payment Coverage Ratio
The fixed charge coverage ratio is very similar to times interest earned. Adding the cost of annual long-term lease obligations to Earnings before Interest and Taxes (EBIT) and dividing this number by the sum of interest charges plus lease obligations produces the result.

Fixed payment coverage ratio = EBIT/interest + (principal payment + lease payments + preferred stock dividend)[1]

This ratio can be particularly important for creditors lending to companies that negotiate long-term leases, since lease payments are both fixed and long term.

Debt Affordability Ratio
Cash inflows and outflows are two important determinants of debt affordability. Cash inflows equal operating income + noncash expenses, while cash outflows pertain to financing costs.

Debt affordability ratio = cash inflows/cash outflows

When debt affordability falls below one, the firm might have taken on too much debt.

Cash Flow Coverage[2]
One of the most important ratios in credit analysis, cash flow coverage, describes the number of times operating cash flows cover debt service. Debt service includes interest and principal. The following example illustrates how computer simulations and cash flow coverage work together.

A builder took his construction plans to Hanover Multifactor Bank requesting $30 million of permanent financing at 5% interest for a 12-year term with a balloon payment due at the end. The constant payment, including interest and principal, would be $3,329,605. The bank stipulated that the building's operating cash flow must be sufficient to cover debt service of $306,900 with no less than a 98% probability. While the builder's net worth statement revealed some liquidity, the bank did not feel comfortable that enough external funds were available to

---

[1] We have not determined the ratio for Jones Designs, Inc.

[2] Not calculated for Jones Designs, Inc.

supplement the project's expected cash flow coverage ratio. The bank ran a simulation. Extracting the cash flow coverage section from the simulation output, the bank determined that because cash flow coverage was good to only an 82.6% probability, short of the 98% required by Hanover Multifactor Bank, collateral and an escrow deposit were required. The customer agreed to the conditions and the bank approved the loan.

Growth Ratios

While strong sales and profit growth rates are generally comforting to lenders, they may well be chimeric. Is growth real or illusionary? Are inflationary factors or noncash credits propelling fiscal results? Are revenues sustainable?

Sales Growth Rate

Sales growth rate $= sales_t - sales_{t-1}/sales_{t-1} = \$586,895 - \$553,675/\$553,675 = 6.0\%$

2013	2014	Industry Average
8.0%	6.0%	9.5%

Profit Growth Rate

Profit growth rate $= profit_t - profit_{t-1}/profit_{t-1} = \$1,965 - \$18,754/\$18,754 = -89.5\%$

2013	2014	Industry Average
−32.9%	−89.5%	11.5%

SOURCES OF COMPARATIVE RATIOS

You can visit numerous sites to obtain comparative ratio information. Some are listed below.

- *Risk Management Association:* The Annual Statement Studies are a source of composite performance metrics derived directly from the financial statements of financial institutions' borrowers and prospects. These financial statements come directly to the RMA from its member institutions, which get their data straight from their customers. It includes Financial Ratio Benchmarks, Industry

Default Probabilities and Cash Flow Measures, and individual NAICS downloads to your spreadsheet.

- *Dun & Bradstreet Key Business Ratios, Financial* helps you to assess how a business is doing compared to an industry or a competitor. The 14 key business ratios cover the critical areas of business performance: solvency, efficiency, and profitability. They are broken down into median figures, with upper and lower quartiles. Ratios are arranged by Standard Industrial Classification (SIC) Codes, a four-digit number that classifies business establishments by defining the industries in which they do business.
- *Compustat North America* is a database of U.S. and Canadian fundamental and market information on active and inactive publicly held companies. It provides more than 300 annual and 100 quarterly income statements, balance sheets, statements of cash flows, and supplemental data items.
- *Compustat Global* is a database of non-U.S. and non-Canadian fundamental and market information on more than 33,900 active and inactive publicly held companies with annual data history from 1987.
- *BizMiner* offers industry financial analysis benchmarks for over 5,000 lines of business, and industry market trends on thousands more. Their market analysis reports are available at the national and local levels down to the zip code. BizMiner is a resource to use when developing business plans, or for any sort of entrepreneurship initiatives in which you need to measure peer performance in an industry.
- *Almanac of Business and Industrial Financial Ratios* provides a data source from tax returns filed with the Internal Revenue Service of the United States. The most recent edition provides data on millions of U.S. corporations. It provides 50 performance indicators for each industry, and at the end of each industry section, performance indicators for the last 10 years are shown. Data are grouped into 13 categories by size of assets in each industry. About 180 lines of business are covered.
- *IRS Corporate Financial Ratios* offer industry ratios based on the most recently available income statement and balance sheet data compiled by the U.S. Internal Revenue Service. There are 79 ratios or averages given for each industry.
- *IBIS World* provides independent, accurate, comprehensive, and up-to-date research on over 700 industries, including statistics,

analysis, and forecasts. While traditional ratios do not appear in the database, IBIS does offer a variety of statistical measures of the industry: executive summary, key statistics, segmentation, market characteristics, industry conditions, key factors, key competitors, industry performance, and outlook.

- *Value Line Investment Survey* is issued weekly in three parts. The index leads the user to the page on which each company report appears, as well as summarizing key data for all 1,700 stocks profiled. Part III, "Ratings and Reports," carries a full-page report on each company, including 15 years or more of summarized balance sheet and income statement data. The core of the analysis appears in the upper left-hand corner, where each stock receives the timeliness rating, the safety rating, and the beta coefficient.

- *The Global Financial Database* is a collection of financial and economic data provided in ASCII or spreadsheet format. There are 20,000 historical or current data series, which may be downloaded directly from the website. Global coverage includes stocks, bonds, Treasury bills, interest rates, commodity prices, CPI, GDP, exchange rates, indexes, population, and more.

- *Mergent Online* offers profiles of public corporations around the world that include summaries, company histories, property, financials, subsidiaries, joint ventures, long-term press releases, and annual reports. PDF images of corporate annual reports for publicly traded foreign corporations and those in the United States are available going back to 1996.

- *Thomson One* features company financials and filings, mergers and acquisition data, and analyst reports. The following types of information are available: company overviews, company news and price charts, corporate governance, corporate financial fundamentals, estimates (and earnings surprises), debt overview, company deals, share ownership information, company research, company financial filings, and officers and directors.

CHAPTER 5

Financing Your Season*

For many small- and medium-sized firms, short-term or working capital loans are used to acquire seasonal assets and are repaid at the end of the cycle by converting inventory and accounts receivable into cash. Seasonal firms are traditionally undercapitalized, requiring short-term financing to support temporary current assets. The cash conversion cycle (or the working capital cycle) is pivotal in the lending process since it focuses on inventory conversion to receivables. Hypothetically, all short-term

---

*Please visit http://booksite.elsevier.com/9780128016985 to view the ancillary material of this chapter.

Navigating the Business Loan. http://dx.doi.org/10.1016/B978-0-12-801698-5.00005-4

debt incurred by the borrower is repaid to the lender at the end of the fiscal period. These credit obligations are satisfied through current asset conversion originally subsidized by a seasonal loan. In basic terms, the working capital cycle describes the cash flow resulting from current asset deployment. Most companies will finance a large portion of working capital by purchasing raw materials on credit, creating accounts payable, and reducing the need for the firm to lay out cash. But this is not enough to support the overall operation.

Seasonal loans are self-liquidating and provide short-term working capital needs by financing seasonal increases in receivables and inventory, the liquidation of which retires the loan at season's end. If the funding is structured properly, a seasonal loan will monitor itself. In other words, both the borrower and lender should know when the loan will peak (full expansion of balance sheet) and when it will be repaid (full contraction of the balance sheet). Any deviation from the *modus operandi* should trigger an immediate inquiry by the lender.

During the year, a seasonal company's balance sheet goes through an expansion and contraction process. At the seasonal high point, or most active part of the period, debt and assets increase to support seasonal activity, thus expanding the balance sheet. During this phase, sales emulate the manufacturing cycle, the result of which is the conversion of inventory into accounts receivables. At the low point, or least active part of the period, the manufacturing cycle has ebbed, leaving the firm with the responsibility to retire outstanding short-term debt. This is accomplished through the conversion of accounts receivables into cash or deposits. Once all short-term debt has been satisfied, a balance sheet will contract back to its normal level. Any excess cash on hand is usually designated for temporary current asset investments next season.

EXAMPLES OF SEASONAL BUSINESSES

- Retail businesses use seasonal loans to support swings in sales activity. Jewelry retailers, bookstores, and toy distributors increase sales markedly just before the holiday season. Retail department stores and candy retailers follow the same pattern. Garden outlets, sporting goods stores, and home lumber dealers experience peak sales during warm spring and summer months. Building contractors, too, achieve higher levels of production when weather is favorable. Clothing stores anticipate increases in volume in the spring and again in the fall as new lines arrive.

- Retail businesses use seasonal loans to support swings in sales activity; retailers tend to borrow heavily during the Christmas and Easter seasons to carry increased inventories and accounts receivable. Swimsuit manufacturers, for example, start producing bathing suits in fall for spring distribution to retailers. During the manufacturing phase, inventories build along with labor, overhead, and other product costs. In the spring swimsuits are sold. Shortly thereafter, receivables fall due, and the proceeds provide the annual loan cleanup.
- Great Lakes steel operations build iron ore inventories during summer months to supply their needs during winter, when lake freighters cannot transport raw materials. Forest products producers build substantial log inventories to keep manufacturing plants supplied with raw materials during seasons when logging operations make little headway. Coal and fuel oil dealers build inventories during summer months, running them off steadily in fall and winter to a low point by early spring. Fish canneries must complete processing as fish are caught, often resulting in accumulation of substantial inventories. Food processors use short-term credit lines to finance crops grown and shipped during particular seasons. Short-term financing supports fertilizer and other production costs and the harvest season for distribution and marketing of the crop.
- Securities commission brokerage and security-trading firms are large short-term bank borrowers. As investment bankers, these firms require short-term funding to support underwriting and distribution activities.

HOW A SUCCESSFUL SEASONAL CYCLE WORKS

The typical seasonal company goes through five stages:

1. *Buildup phase:* Bank deposits drop, whereas loan balances, trade payables, and inventory increase. The balance sheet begins to expand.
2. *High point phase:* Inventory, bank debt, and trade payables reach a peak. The need for liquidity bottoms out, and receivables remain

low. The balance sheet reaches expansion limits. In part due to heavy inventory requirements, borrowers are usually undercapitalized.

3. *Asset conversion cycle begins:* Inventory reduces as accounts receivables expand. Accounts payables and bank debt remain unchanged or decline slightly. The balance sheet moves in tandem with the reduction in liabilities.

4. *Conversion cycle intensifies:* Shipments accelerate, triggering further inventory reductions, while receivables continue to build. Demand deposits rise as some receivables convert to cash. Payables and short-term loans begin to reduce as balance sheet contraction moves in tandem with cash conversion.

5. *Conversion cycle subsides:* The low point approaches and firms ship very little merchandise. Inventory is at low levels and receivables decline quickly, since the conversion process causes bank deposits to swell. Cash rich, seasonal borrowers clean up short-term lines and retire remaining trade payables. All is ready to duplicate the process next season.

UNSUCCESSFUL SEASONAL CYCLES

Sometimes things go wrong – order bookings fall well below the corresponding period last year, backlogs go unsatisfied, finished products disappoint customers and go unsold, and competitors enter the market offering better deals. Here is the typical unsuccessful scenario.

1. *Buildup phase:* Demand deposits drop and loan balances, trade payables and inventory increase. The balance sheet starts expanding. So far, so good.

2. *High point phase:* As the firm reaches its high point, inventory, bank debt, and trade payables peak. Liquidity requirements abate, receivables remain low, and the balance sheet reaches expansion limits. Still no observable signs of trouble.

3. *Conversion cycle fails:* Surprises come fast – bookings are canceled, goods ship late, production breakdowns occur, and consumer demand evaporates. With inventory stuck at high levels, receivables and cash fail to expand, the result of an impeded conversion cycle.

4. With low cash balances, borrowers find it difficult or impossible to repay suppliers and short-term lenders.

The big question is: Was the unsuccessful season a temporary or structural problem? Minor setbacks, like the common cold, do not disturb lenders. Firms make mistakes occasionally, and then hop right back on track. Serious illnesses, so to speak, are a different story. Here is how diagnosis works: if, at the end of the day, a firm's receivables portfolio has all but disappeared, lenders deduce serious structural problems and quite possibly will think the loan will not work out.

EXAMPLES OF SUCCESSFUL SEASONAL CYCLES

Acme Toy Company typically receives orders for the bulk of its sales during the summer months. Shipments of orders are expected in October, November, and December, just in time for the start of the holiday rush. Since Acme manufactures most of its product line before the shipping period, short-term bank loans are used to finance raw material buildup. As toys are delivered to retailers during the fall months, the firm experiences higher receivable levels as inventory is sold. After the holiday season ends, inventory and receivables decline as deposits increase. Cash is used to pay down short-term bank loans and payables. As long as the firm sells inventory, debt and equity levels normalize by fiscal close, and the firm's short-term undercapitalized position is just that: *temporary*.

Gem Lawn Furniture closes its books on August 31. During late summer and fall, Gem purchases raw materials, the bulk of which are forest product derivatives, and seasonal borrowing begins. Labor and other manufacturing costs increase during late fall and early winter, pushing borrowings to a high point. By late winter demand accelerates, with products shipped from warehouses to distribution channels. Inventories reduce while receivables increase. With production at or near a low point, Gem's credit line levels off. By early summer, receivables and bank debt begin running off, the result of cash collections. At the close of books August 31, inventories and receivables reduce to their annual low point and seasonal debt is retired.

The successful conversion contraction flow experienced by Gem may not have occurred if short-term debt were used to finance long-duration or core assets (as opposed to seasonal assets) because the firm would be forced to use cash to pay two short-term loans simultaneously. Core assets ideally are financed with long-term debt (match funding) to maintain working capital needed to clean up seasonal loans. Core assets (nonseasonal) are a firm's nerve center, its most direct route to sustainable cash flows and shareholder value. Remember that at a seasonal low point or fiscal close date, seasonal assets all but disappear on a balance sheet. All that remains are core assets. Core assets are supported by liabilities of similar duration. Short-term debt used to finance core assets could easily result in seasonal liquidity problems.

SEASONAL LENDING ANALYSIS

One of the best ways to determine when peak requirements occur is cash budget analysis. Cash budgets reveal seasonal assets' buildup periods along with the likelihood that advances funding seasonal operations will be repaid. Lender and borrower alike determine at what stages cash infusions are needed during the seasonal build-up phase and at precisely what stage cash inflows outflank outflows. Cash budgets range from short periods – monthly, quarterly, semiannually, or annually – to long-term strategic plans covering periods beyond a year. Cash budgets are indispensable short-term lending tools.

PREPARING A CASH BUDGET (REFER TO ACME'S CASH BUDGET)[1]

While cash budgets usually span short periods – monthly, quarterly, semiannually, annually – management will also use cash budgets to help bring into focus long-term horizons of 2, 5, or 10 years.

Cash budgets' benefits to lenders are the following:

• Cash budgets enable lenders to monitor seasonal build-up outflows along with low-point inflows. For instance, if actual cash receipts fall short of projections (month-to-month comparatives), sluggish sales, distribution, or product problems may be at fault. You will have a difficult time blaming economic actual versus projected variances if competitor firms are stable.

---

[1] Illustrative Example: Acme Toy Company Excel Cash Budget
Location: Excel workbook is available on the Elsevier Website, at www.ElsevierDirect.com.
Brief Description: Typical cash budget used in the analysis of seasonal loans

- Cash budgets help lenders establish optimal credit lines. Lenders traditionally set seasonal credit lines to approximate the largest deficit (financial requirement) demonstrated.
- Cash budgets show when repayment is likely. Firms requesting additional funds at times when loan balances should be decreasing should have a good reason for the request. In all likelihood the cash conversion cycle collapsed.
- Cash budgets identify wayward deployment of seasonal advances. For example, if a borrower suffered a fiscal loss and anticipates payment of substantial dividends, the loan may be used to line investors' pockets and not to finance seasonal working capital. Borrowers have also been known to fund the activities of affiliates or management-sponsored investments out of loans bankers intended for the purchase of inventory. Make sure you have a good explanation if "advances to affiliates" shows up in your cash budget.
- Capital expenditures may point to large cash disbursements. Time and again, lenders spot planned capital outlays, and propose term loans and revolving credit, thus taking pressure off seasonal balance sheets. In this instance, the cash budget even works as a sales tool, drumming up added business.
- Cash budgets provide a window through which lenders anticipate cash surpluses. Anticipated surpluses might be invested in a managed investment account.
- Cash budgets work as quasi-marketing tools. For instance, capital expenditures normally call for considerable cash outlays during the budget period. Lenders see these outlays as business opportunities. If they spot anticipated outlays early enough, they may offer term loans or other facilities.

EXERCISE: PREPARING A CASH BUDGET

Refer to Table 5.1, Acme's cash budget.

1. Acme has requested a $7.5 million credit line to support seasonal operations.
2. Set up a matrix that includes both historical and forecast sales by month. Data can be extracted from the obligor's projected sales

Table 5.1 Acme Total Cash Inflows

Acme Toy Company
Cash Budget
3/31/2014
(in 000's up to decimal point)

	Actual Sales				Forecasted Sales					
	December	January	February	March	April	May	June	July	August	September
Total Sales	900.00	900.00	1,800.00	2,250.00	2,700.00	3,600.00	5,400.00	5,400.00	2,700.00	1,800.00
Credit Sales	45.00	63.00	90.00	180.00	225.00	450.00	1,575.00	1,575.00	135.00	45.00
Cash Sales					2,475.00	3,150.00	3,825.00	3,825.00	2,565.00	1,755.00
First Month (A)					56.25	112.50	393.75	393.75	33.75	11.25
Second Month (B)					9.00	11.25	22.50	78.75	78.75	6.75
Third Month (C)					36.90	73.80	92.25	184.50	645.75	645.75
Fourth Month (D)					5.67	8.10	16.20	20.25	40.50	141.75
Total Cash Receipts Forecasted from Sales and Collections					2,582.82	3,355.65	4,349.70	4,502.25	3,363.75	2,560.50
(A) Percent of Current Month's Credit Sales	25.00%									
(B) Percent of Prior Month's Credit Sales	5.00%									
(C) Percent of Second Prior Month's Credit Sales	41.00%									
(D) Percent of Third Prior Month's Credit Sales	9.00%									
Total Cash Receipts Forecasted from Sales and Collections					2,582.82	3,355.65	4,349.70	4,502.25	3,363.75	2,560.50
Cash Dividends Received					45.00			45.00		
Disposals							540.00			
Interest					9.00	9.00	9.00	9.00	9.00	9.00
Total Cash Inflow					2,636.82	3,364.65	4,898.70	4,556.25	3,372.75	2,569.50

budget, which projects the expected monthly sales in units and selling price per unit.

3. Next, calculate credit sales as a percent of total sales. Acme sells 80% on credit.
4. Subtract credit sales from total sales to arrive at credit sales.
5. Next, develop an accounts receivable aging from historical experience and expectations. For example, Acme expects 25% of present month's credit sales will be collected in the current month, and 5% of prior month's credit sales to be collected in the current month.
6. Enter expected collections in the budget you have developed from the aging.
7. Enter total cash inflows.
8. Develop the cash disbursement for purchases schedule following the same method we used to find cash receipts from sales.
9. Enter total cash inflows.
10. Juxtapose total cash inflows with outflows.
11. Complete cumulative (financial needs) surplus zero balance account matrix. This schedule assumes that the firm keeps no minimum balance and that First City Bank will automatically finance all overdrafts.
12. Complete the cash budget assuming Acme requires a minimum $900 in their demand deposit account at all times.

Acme Toy Company will require $1,210,680 in April and $147,600 in May. Loan balances reduce during June and are followed by cash surpluses through September. This firm does not need a $7.5 million credit line as $1.2 million is the maximum budget deficit. Therefore, $1.5 million to $2 million loan amounts appear to satisfy the requirements of the budget (Table 5.2).

INTERIM SEASONAL RATIO ANALYSIS

As we saw earlier, lenders must decide whether they have sufficient information to perform proper due diligence. In more than a few cases, small- and medium-sized companies may not have the ability (or inclination) to supply year-to-date financial information on the spot. At this point, it takes an experienced lender to decide on the required information, crunch the numbers, prepare a write-up, and follow progress from last fiscal date to the interim (Table 5.3).

Table 5.2 Acme Total Cash Outflows

Cash Disbursements for Purchases

	Actual Purchases				Forecasted Purchases					
	December	January	February	March	April	May	June	July	August	September
Total					900.00	900.00	450.00	225.00	225.00	270.00
Credit	2,700.00	2,700.00	1,350.00	900.00	900.00	900.00	225.00	225.00	225.00	270.00
Cash	1,800.00	1,800.00	1,350.00	900.00	0.00	0.00	225.00	45.00	45.00	90.00
Payment										
First Month (A)					225.00	225.00	56.25	11.25	11.25	22.50
Second Month (B)					558.00	558.00	558.00	139.50	27.90	27.90
Third Month (C)					148.50	99.00	99.00	99.00	24.75	4.95
Fourth Month (D)					27.00	20.25	13.50	13.50	13.50	3.38
Total Cash Disbursements Forecasted from Purchases					958.50	902.25	951.75	443.25	257.40	238.73

(A) Percent of Current Month's Credit Purchases	25.00%
(B) Percent of Prior Month's Credit Purchases	62.00%
(C) Percent of Second Prior Month's Credit Purchases	11.00%
(D) Percent of Third Prior Month's Credit Purchases	1.50%

Total Cash Disbursements

	April	May	June	July	August	September
Selling Expenses	958.50	902.25	951.75	443.25	257.40	238.73
General and Administration Expenses	765.00	900.00	1,080.00	1,080.00	540.00	360.00
Taxes: Income	1,350.00	1,620.00	1,530.00	1,350.00	1,350.00	1,350.00
Taxes: Withholding	126.00			126.00		
Pensions	90.00	90.00	90.00	90.00	90.00	90.00
Dividends	45.00		45.00		45.00	
Funded Debt Payments	63.00			63.00		
Other Outflows	450.00			450.00		
Total Cash Outflow	3,847.50	3,512.25	3,696.75	3,602.25	2,282.40	2,038.73

Table 5.3 Juxtaposing Total Cash Inflows to Total Cash Outflows

	April	May	June	July	August	September
Total Cash In	2,636.82	3,364.65	4,898.70	4,556.25	3,372.75	2,569.50
Total Cash Out	3,847.50	3,512.25	3,696.75	3,602.25	2,282.40	2,038.73
Net Cash Available	(1,210.68)	(147.60)	1,201.95	954.00	1,090.35	530.78
Cumulative Cash Available	(1,210.68)	(1,358.28)	(156.33)	797.67	1,888.02	2,418.80

	April	May	June	July	August	September
Net Cash Available	(1,210.68)	(147.60)	1,201.95	954.00	1,090.35	530.78
Cash Balance Available (Balance March 31)	900.00	(310.68)	(458.28)	743.67	1,697.67	2,788.02
Cumulative (Financial Needs) Surplus Zero Balance Account	(310.68)	(458.28)	743.67	1,697.67	2,788.02	3,318.80
Minimum Cash Balance	900.00	900.00	900.00	900.00	900.00	900.00
Cumulative (Financial Needs) Minimum Balance	(1,210.68)	(1,358.28)	(156.33)	797.67	1,888.02	2,418.80

The ability to expand and contract a balance sheet during seasonal high and low points offers assurance of a productive season. Smart lenders obtain interim reports monthly or quarterly on a case-by-case basis, compute interim (seasonal) ratios to confirm satisfactory asset conversion, and compare results (June of the present year matched to June of the prior year, for example). Let us revisit Jones Designs, Inc. with respect to seasonal ratio due diligence. Partial financials appear below:

Jones Designs, Inc.
Fractional Balance Sheet
Year Ended December 31
($ Thousands)

	2012	2013	2014
Current Assets			
Cash and cash items	15,445	12,007	11,717
Accounts and notes receivable, net	51,793	55,886	88,571
Inventories	56,801	99,087	139,976
Current Assets	124,039	166,980	240,264
Current Liabilities			
Short-term loans	10,062	15,800	55,198
Accounts payable	20,292	31,518	59,995
Accruals	10,328	15,300	21,994
Current Liabilities	40,682	62,618	137,187

(Cash + Accounts Receivable)/(Short-Term Bank Debt + Trade Payables)

2014	$(11,717 + 88,571)/(55,198 + 59,995) = .87$
2013	$(12,007 + 55,886)/(15,800/31,518) = 1.43$

Near the seasonal low point, cash and receivables should be sufficient to reduce short-term debt and trade payables. Watch for a drop in shipments or slow receivables if the ratio falls below historical levels. This firm's liquid position is markedly weaker than the corresponding period last year.

	2012	2013	2014
Gross sales	529,393	580,375	638,485
Returns and allowances	(16,700)	(26,700)	(51,590)
Net Sales	512,693	553,675	586,895
Cost of goods sold	(405,803)	(450,394)	(499,928)
Gross profit	106,890	103,281	86,967
Gross profit margin	20.8%	18.7%	14.8%

Returns Allowances and Discounts/Gross Sales

2014	51,590/638,485 = 8.1%
2013	26,700/580,375 = 4.6%
2011	16,700/529,393 = 3.2%

The jump in returns may be the result of defective merchandise already shipped or goods shipped after the season. The firm's creditors are certain to ask if merchandise was reshipped and accepted. Seasonal inventories held post season are ripe for write–downs, are barometers of quality, and will not be taken lightly.

Short-Term Bank Debt/Trade Payables

2014	55,198/59,995 = 92.0%
2013	15,800/31,518 = 50.1%
2012	10,062/20,292 = 49.6%

This seasonal ratio goes hand in hand with:

Trade inquiries November and December, reported separately

2014	55
2013	16
2012	12

Trade inquiries should be compared alongside short-term bank debt to payables. Recall that early stages of asset conversion bring about elevated debt levels. Thus, suppliers seek out credit information before shipping raw materials, flooding creditors with inquiries. Normally, trade inquiries reduce dramatically following a peak-season high point. Experienced lenders keep a list of inquiries, recording the date, supplier, reason for the inquiry, and comments. Unreasonably high bank-to-trade debt ratios coming on the heels of an excessive volume of inquiries post season suggest suppliers are worried because they haven't been paid. They call the bank to check if the firm is still viable, then contact the firm and insist on immediate payment, or plan next season's raw materials to be shipped on cash-on-demand terms. The firm then calls its bank to borrow enough to close supplier debts during the post season – the period not to borrow, the time when the obligor should be cash rich! Short-term bank debt/trade payables combined with a tally of supplier bank inquiries approaching the end of the seasonal cycle helps to avoid this unfortunate loan exposure.

Purchases/Sales

A sharp purchases increase relative to sales points to inventory overload. The buildup might be a byproduct of unwise inventory management, or simply to gear up in anticipation of orders. Purchase figures were *not* available.

Breakeven Shipments Formula

Developed by this author, the breakeven shipments formula is most useful from the first days of the shipping season until season's end. Shipments must be sufficient to cover production and operating expenses incurred during a seasonal cycle. If the breakeven shipment levels fall short, losses will be incurred, perhaps even substantial fiscal losses. For example, seasonal firms that struggle to break even during shipment months, when expenses are low and sales high, cannot easily offset buildup period outlays. Suppliers' and lenders' obligations, agreed to earlier in the season, will likely remain unpaid.

Breakeven shipments formula

$$S_b = E_i/(G_i)(1-R_i)$$

where:

S_b = Breakeven shipments
E_i = Estimated expenses in the shipment month or months
G_i = Interim gross profit margin estimated or actual in shipment month or months
R_i = (returns + allowances + sales)/gross sales
S_e = Shipments expected during the month(s)

Compare S_b to S_e,

If $S_e > S_b$ Profits
If $S_e < S_b$ Losses
If $S_e = S_b$ Breakeven

A borrower provides the following information for the month of April:

Estimated gross profit margin: 35%
Estimated shipments: $500,000
Returns allowances and discounts: 10% of gross sales
Expected expenses for April: $200,000

$S_b = E_i/(G_i)(1-R_i)$
$S_b = 200,000/(.35)(1-.10)$
$S_b = 634,900$

Since estimated shipments of $500,000 ($S_e$) fall below breakeven $634,000 ($S_b$), the seasonal firm will incur a loss during the month of April.

DEFENSIVE MEASURES

While storm signals come in all shapes and sizes, the big question is: Are problems temporary or structural? Leading credit-related red flags are reviewed in Chapter 1. Seasonal loan defensive measures protect lenders before red flags are hoisted.

Prudently structured seasonal credits ostensibly fall back on a second way out, which is a good exit strategy. Minor temporary problems generally call for simply waiving annual cleanups. If problems are serious, creditors may decide to restructure loans by advancing term loan or revolvers, repaid over subsequent years out of operating cash flows. Loan agreements, written with robust covenants, and events of default, offer creditors greater control. Consider these factors:

- *Cash flow:* Strong cash flows customarily make it to debt service (interest plus principal payments). If established seasonal borrowers boast exceptional historical track records, creditors can afford to be generous because healthy cash flows promised over the next 1 or 2 years will offset this year's (temporary) seasonal setbacks. However, lenders expect that bleak cash flows expected down the road will turn a current year inventory setback into to chronic structural problems. We cover cash flow analysis in Chapter 6.

- *Equity injection:* Owners may be asked to inject cash in the form of subordinated debt or straight equity if poor operating cash flow depletes equity capital, or if assets are poorly utilized.
- *Formula-based advances:* Advances made against confirmed orders, or asset liens, may work on a temporary basis (see Chapter 8).
- *Credit insurance:* Insurance against excessive losses may be assigned to the bank, but only viable firms may apply. Credit insurance is unavailable or prohibitively expensive if obligors are in trouble.

WORKING CAPITAL AS A DEFENSIVE MEASURE

Broadly defined, working capital is the excess of current assets over current liabilities. Working capital is cash and other assets expected to be consumed or converted into cash over the accounting period, less obligations due during the same period. Working capital is a generic measure of liquidity acting as the margin of protection that short-term creditors depend on behind the conversion of current assets. In short, basic understanding of working capital mechanics offers lenders a methodology whereby they can differentiate between temporary and structural problems.

CASH FLOW VERSUS WORKING CAPITAL ANALYSIS

A cash flow[2] is more refined than a working capital analysis and should be employed to evaluate loans with maturities beyond 1 year. However, working capital solutions are more direct and perfectly suited for seasonal "what's my second way out?" assessment.

THE MECHANICS OF WORKING CAPITAL

Simple, very useful working capital math (Table 5.4) crystallizes the flow of funds approach, pointing the way to a second way out of a seasonal imbalance.

---

[2] Covered in Chapter 6.

Table 5.4 Working Capital Arithmetic		
Equation	Equation Defined	Explanation
5.1	Assets = liabilities + equity	Basic accounting equation
5.2	Working capital = current assets − current liabilities	Traditional working capital definition
5.3	Current assets + fixed assets = current liabilities + fixed liabilities + equity	Equation (5.1) expanded
5.4	Current assets − current liabilities = fixed liabilities + equity − fixed assets	Rearrange current accounts to the left of the equal sign and noncurrent accounts to the right.
5.5	Working capital = fixed liabilities + equity − fixed assets	Substitution: Equation (5.2) equals Equation (5.4)
5.6	ΔWorking capital = Δfixed liabilities + Δequity − Δfixed assets	Increases in working capital depend on increases in fixed liabilities, increases in equity, and decreases in fixed assets.
5.7	− ΔWorking capital = − Δfixed liabilities − Δequity + Δfixed assets	Decreases in working capital are a function of decreases in fixed liabilities, decreases in equity, and increases in fixed assets.
5.8	Working capital + fixed assets = fixed liabilities + equity	Rearrange equation by moving fixed assets to the left of the equal sign.

From Equation (5.6) in Table 5.4 we see that subtracting the noncurrent accounts of two balance sheets is equal to working capital. Thus, increases in noncurrent liabilities, increases in equity, and reductions in noncurrent assets denote sources of funds. From Equation (5.7) we see that decreases in noncurrent liabilities, decreases in equity, and increases in noncurrent assets serve as uses of working capital. The concepts in Equations (5.6) and (5.7) are known and appeared in financial statements prior to the Statement of Financial Accounting Standards No. 95, "Statement of Cash Flows" (November 1987).

Be familiar with Equation (5.8) because it opens the door to a seasonal loan's exit strategy, that is, a replacement long-term loan (temporary seasonal setbacks will not become structural, or long term). Accordingly, Equation (5.8) represents the core of working capital liquidity analysis. The right side of Equation (5.8) − long-term liabilities (generally funded debt) plus equity − embodies the firm's capital structure, or permanent financing. Equation (5.8) proves that the capital structure supports both fixed assets plus a firm's working capital (liquidity) position. For example, suppose a banker lent money to a business only to find out that because of structural problems (competitive pressures, eroding gross profit margin, etc.) the obligor will at best break even. Assuming no new stock is issued, the equity component of the capital structure decreases or in a best-case offering remains constant.

Next, since a major new debt attractor is continuous expansion of the equity base, the firm may find it difficult to attract debt capital. The right side of Equation (5.8) will reduce or remain unchanged at best. Let us assume capital expenditures are bottlenecked because the major part of the capital expansion program the bank financed has been poorly deployed. If the fixed asset component balloons upward while the capital structure stagnates or falls, lenders will likely lose liquidity protection, or find the proverbial second way out of the credit.

On the other hand, suppose the borrower promises strong, quality profits over the next few years. The firm will likely prosper and draw on its long-term financing sources. The capital structure will indeed expand. And if fixed assets are maintained at efficient levels, the working capital component in Equation (5.8) expands nicely. Liquidity flows into the business to finance innovative product lines, reduce debt levels, help fund acquisitions, and position the balance sheet for high-yield restructuring, leveraged buyouts, and Treasury stock purchases. Equation (5.8) provides a straightforward methodology for working capital (funds) analysis. Equation (5.8) math points to three factors that produce liquidity levels short-term lenders look to for protection. If your lender fails to address these concepts, remind your lender – as long as the factors work in your favor. Simply keep in mind that sustainable liquidity hinges on (1) strong, attainable, and retained profits, enough to cover debt service; (2) optimal match funding whereby obligors borrow in the long term to finance long-term assets and in the short term to carry a season; (3) ensuring fixed assets are productive and produce industry-acceptable internal rates of return.

Many firms unsuited for unsecured seasonal borrowings may meet financing needs by securing assets or changing over to accounts receivable financing discussed in Chapter 8. Collateral and accounts receivable financing will be discussed in relation to risk characteristics of the borrower, advantages to the borrower and creditor, credit and collateral analysis, documentation, and safeguards that help ensure the authenticity and collectability of assigned collateral. Remember collateral is like frosting on a pound cake. Collateral will not automatically assure payment; collateralized lenders judge overall risks by evaluating the quality and magnitude of collateral, the borrower's financial condition, management's strategic plans, cash flow, and debt servicing ability.

Exploring Your Business's Nerve Center: Cash Flow*,1

OUTLINE

HISTORICAL CASH FLOW[1]

Cash flow is your firm's lifeblood. It means, literally, cash flowing through a business during the course of a fiscal year. Lenders say that cash flow analysis may be the most important tool in their repertoire, the tool by which commercial and investment bankers evaluate loans and value companies. A cash flow statement will highlight your firm's activities in a way that an income statement will not. Through cash flow statements, experienced lenders figure out, before they approve an extension or a

---

*Please visit http://booksite.elsevier.com/9780128016985 to view the ancillary material of this chapter.

[1]Readers are encouraged to read Chapter 6, Cash Flow Analysis, in a book written by Glantz, M, Mun, J. Credit Engineering for Bankers, A Practical Guide for Bank Lending, 2nd ed. Elsevier, 2011. Topics include introduction to analysis, indirect and direct methods of cash reporting, the banker's cash flow, and reconciliations including equity, net fixed asset, long-term debt, investments, deferred taxes, and minority interest. Additional topics include the four-step approach required to build a banker's cash flow from scratch and cash flow constituent points.

Navigating the Business Loan. http://dx.doi.org/10.1016/B978-0-12-801698-5.00006-6

new facility, how efficiently and profitably customers used prior loans. Without cash flow statements, lenders have an incomplete picture of the business simply because accounting entries alone do not reveal both the degree to which historical and future cash flows cover debt service and borrowers' chances for survival. Credit-worthy, low-volatile operating cash flows point to reduced default probabilities. On the other hand, lenders view weak, unreliable operating cash flow and increasing, elevated default probabilities as two peas in the same pod. For example, low default probabilities are linked to three cash flow attributes:

1. Cash flow *quality:* cash flow absent of shenanigans, inflated earnings, and problematic noncash charges and credits
2. Cash flow *magnitude:* optimal balance between internally generated cash and financing activities
3. Cash flow *trend:* dependable, improved earnings contributing to value-added internal cash flow

We will assess two cash flow structures: standardized cash flow and the banker's cash flow.

The Standardized Cash Flow Statement[2]

The objective of the standard indirect method is to focus on information dealing with historical changes in cash and cash equivalents by means of a statement of cash flow, which categorizes cash flows during fiscal periods from operating, investing, and financing activities. The presentation of this statement begins with operating activities: net income or loss, additions to or deductions from net income, changes in receivables, inventory, payables, accruals, and other related accounts.

The separate disclosure of cash flows arising from investing activities is important because the cash flows represent the extent to which expenditures have been made for resources intended to generate future income and support future cash flows. Expenditures that result in a recognized asset in the statement of financial position are highlighted for classification as investing activities. Examples of cash flows arising from investing activities include cash payments to acquire property, plant and equipment, intangibles, and other long-term assets; cash receipts from sales of property, plant and equipment, intangibles, and other long-term assets;

---

[2]International Accounting Standard 7, EC staff consolidated version as of March 24, 2010.

cash advances and loans made to other parties; and cash receipts from the repayment of advances and loans made to other parties.

Separate disclosure of cash flows arising from financing activities is crucial because it often predicts claims on future cash flows by providers of capital to the entity. Cash flows arising from financing activities include cash proceeds from issuing shares or other equity instruments; cash payments to owners to acquire or redeem the entity's shares (Treasury stock); cash proceeds from issuing debentures, loans, notes, bonds, mortgages, and other short- or long-term borrowings; and cash repayments of amounts borrowed. The indirect method of presentation is widespread because the information required is relatively easily assembled from the accounts that a business normally maintains. The standardized cash flow statement is represented in Exhibit 6.1.

The standardized cash flow statement combines working capital assets/liabilities and gross operating cash flow (GOCF) entries, which is, unfortunately, not the optimal form of disclosure. Net operating cash

Operating Activities		
Net Income	102,000	
Depreciation	120,000	
Deferred Tax Credits	(1,600)	
Equity Earnings in Unconsolidated Subsidiaries	(34,000)	
Increase in Accounts Receivable	(123,000)	
Increase in Inventory	(54,000)	
Decrease in Accounts Payable	(69,000)	
Increase in Accrued Expenses	<u>12,000</u>	
Net Cash Provided by Operating Activities		**(47,600)**
Investment Activities		
Purchase of Equipment	(300,000)	
Decrease in Notes Receivable	15,000	
Disposals	<u>11,000</u>	
Total Investment Activities		**(274,000)**
Financing Activities		
Increase in Long-Term Notes Payable	378,000	
Increases in Short-Term Debt	72,000	
New Equity	<u>20,000</u>	
Total Financing Activities		<u>**470,000**</u>
Change in Cash		**148,400**
Cash at beginning of the period		3,000
Cash at end of the period		151,400

Exhibit 6.1. The Standardized Cash Flow Statement

flow (which we discuss shortly) cannot be appraised appropriately if working capital accounts comingle with income statement items. GOCF represents income's ability to provide primary internal cash necessary for future growth and to attract financing. Furthermore, cash flow statements found in annual reports, that is, the reporting line *net cash provided by operating activities*, mix income statement entries with balance sheet accounts. Income-generated cash is therefore undisclosed. Loans are repaid with cash, not earnings. Moreover, cash provided by operating activities combines operating working capital with earnings. For example, earnings after taxes, noncash charges and credits, accounts receivable, inventory, payables, and accruals are not segregated into appropriate groupings. You deserve the best, so it is advisable to ask your accountant to convert the standard cash flow statement into the banker's form before you apply for credit or seek investors.

The Banker's Cash Flow Statement

We classify actual cash flowing from the income statement as gross operating cash flow (GOCF). GOCF ties into *cash provided by debt financing activities*, making it easier for lenders to check imbalances between internal and external financing in order to appraise your firm's financial leverage magnitude and trend. The banker's cash flow (Exhibit 6.2) becomes a critical element in the due diligence process because it depicts changes in cash far more meticulously than standard cash flows (Exhibit 6.1), and unveils an obligor's ability to generate enough cash to meet its obligations, thereby assessing the soundness of a company's liquidity and solvency position.

Large profits do not necessarily point to healthy cash flows. Some lenders assume, incorrectly, that large profits definitively mean an obligor firm is doing well. Profits can be easily manipulated by window dressing. Unlike standard cash flows, our banker's cash flow reveals tangible cash income, making it easier for lenders to differentiate between firms that actually bring in the cash and produce real profits as opposed to firms that window dress or otherwise manipulate profits. Finally, financial ratios go hand-in-hand with the banker's cash flow statement to provide a better understanding of the stories behind the numbers. We will start by examining gross operating cash flow and move down the document.

Operating Activities		
Net Income	102,000	–
Plus/Less: Non-cash Items		
Depreciation	120,000	–
Deferred Tax Credits	(1,600)	–
Equity Earnings in Unconsolidated Subsidiary	(34,000)	–
Gross Operating Cash Flow		186,400
Operating Cash Needs		
Increase in Accounts Receivable	(123,000)	–
Increase in Inventory	(54,000)	(177,000)
Operating Cash Sources		
Decrease in Accounts Payable	(69,000)	–
Increase in Accrued Expenses	12,000	(57,000)
Net Cash Provided by Operating Activities		(47,600)
Investment Activities		
Purchase of Equipment	(300,000)	–
Decrease in Notes Receivable	15,000	–
Disposals	11,000	–
Total Investment Activities		(274,000)
Financing Activities		
Increase in Long-Term Notes Payable	378,000	–
Increase in Short-Term Debt	72,000	–
New Equity	20,000	–
Total Financing Activities		470,000
Change in Cash		148,400
Cash at beginning of the period		3,000
Cash at end of the period		151,400

Exhibit 6.2. The Banker's Cash Flow Statement

Gross Operation Cash Flow (GOCF)

Operating Activities		
Net Income	102,000	–
Plus/less: noncash items		
Depreciation	120,000	–
Deferred tax credits	(1,600)	–
Equity earnings in unconsolidated subsidiary	(34,000)	–
Gross operating cash flow	–	186,400

Gross operating cash flow, as we mentioned, is a key feature of the banker's cash flow. It represents cash that actually appeared on the fiscal income statement. Lenders consider GOCF the primary source of internal financing because it is the sum of net income plus noncash charges, less noncash credits, plus or minus nonoperating events. This section depicts cash generated by operating income, usually the borrower's dominant source of internal financing. Noncash charges represent reductions in income that do not call for cash outlays. Depreciation and amortization, provision for deferred taxes, asset write-downs, and amortization of bond discounts, provisions, reserves, and losses in equity investments are familiar examples of noncash charges. Noncash credits increase earnings without generating cash and include equity earnings in unconsolidated investments, amortization of bond premiums, and negative deferred tax provisions. Nonoperating charges and earnings such as restructuring gains/charges and gains and losses on the sale of equipment are adjusted as well, representing further refinements to reported earnings.

A typical interpretative problem is disclosure of unconsolidated entities in which cash inflows depend on dividend streams returned by projects or investment divestitures. Noncash profits can easily be managed by selecting liberal accounting methods or by simply manufacturing income. If any of the following operating cash flow traps appears in your cash flow statement, be prepared to discuss them with you lender or potential investor:

1. Before you arrive at a loan or investment interview, be prepared to talk over the quality, magnitude, and trend of your firm's earnings.
2. Merchandise is sometimes shipped out at the end of the year to window dress financials.
3. Your creditor will be on the lookout for the following warning signs: unearned income; shifting sales to future periods via reserves; income-smoothing gimmicks; creating gains and losses by selling or retiring debt; hiding losses inside discontinued operations; moving current expenses to later periods by improperly capitalizing costs; amortizing costs too slowly; and failing to write off worthless assets. Be on the lookout for these warning signs, and if necessary, prepare a convincing explanation.
4. When you analyze your firm's earnings trends, pay particular attention to net income's contribution to overall financing. If income contributes less and less to overall financing, recheck your business or strategic plans and prepare an effective defense.
5. Run a dividend payout test: divide net income by dividends. Are dividends paid to investors generous relative to earnings?

6. Compare depreciation expense to capital expenditures. If over the years depreciation expense trends were higher than capital expenditures, fixed assets may be running down and may be well below optimal levels. The firm's gross margin will tell the tale since capital expenditures are reflected as a fixed cost included in cost of goods sold and gross profit. Disappointing gross profit margins are sure to catch your lender's eye, but more importantly, should stimulate you to straighten out your business.

7. While reserves and write-downs such as inventory write-downs are add-backs to gross operating cash flow, these entries are problematic and will be debated during loan interviews.

8. Cash generated from nonrecurring items may artificially inflate your profits, but these items cannot be depended upon to provide sustainable cash flows. One-time extraordinary expenses rarely impact long-term cash flows. Gains and losses from the sale of business units, judgments awarded, and other one-time cash inflows serve as examples. For example, if XYZ, Inc. settles a lawsuit over patent infringement, the firm's long-term health will likely not be affected if XYZ can afford the settlement. On the other hand, consider a pharmaceutical company that loses a product liability suit, resulting in a cash settlement along with the recall of its best-selling drug. If the product is crucial to long-term survival, the borrower may end up financially distressed. Lenders have been through all this before. Nonrecurring items should not influence credit decisions, simply because core earnings pay off loans, not phantom events. Indeed, your borrowings or capital stock issues may provide more funds than operations, but you can be sure lenders count on your successful, profitable business to provide the funds to help finance ongoing operations, repay obligations, and distribute dividends.

9. Equity earnings show up on the income statement as increases to earnings. These often-illusory earnings end up in retained earnings, and because they are noncash items, leverage and coverage ratios may be distorted. What is the story behind equity earning? Suppose your firm owns between 20% and 50% of another firm's stock. Accounting standards say your firm "influences" the other firm's operations, requiring your accountant to include the prorated share of earnings in your own firm's financial statements. Thus,

if the other firm makes $1,000,000 profit, 25% of those profits (or $250,000) will be included in your fiscal statement as equity earnings in unconsolidated subsidiaries.

10. Deferred tax credits cause earnings to increase but may not provide cash or offer a sustainable source of cash. Deferred tax credits often come about when previous provisions for deferred taxes are reversed.

Operating Cash Needs

Operating Cash Needs		
Increase in accounts receivable	(123,000)	—
Increase in inventory	(54,000)	(177,000)

Operating cash needs include increases and decreases in operating current assets. Of approximately equal magnitude, accounts receivable and inventory typically constitute almost 80% of current assets in manufacturing industries. With such a large, relatively volatile working capital investment, operating cash needs deserve special attention. Accounts receivable and inventory levels reflect marketing abilities and credit policies. Revenue from sales may have been reported for the period, but cash may not have been received. A rise in receivables represents a use of cash and is usually financed. A decrease in receivables is associated with cash inflows.

Beware of the following red flags, and if they exist, prepare a good explanation before meeting with your lender: large overdue receivables; excessive dependence on one or two customers; related-party receivables; slow receivables turnover; existing right of return; changes in terms, credit standards, discounts, or collections; or creating receivables through distortive accounting. If the average collection period (ACP) increased, know the reason or reasons for the change. Recall from Chapter 4, that the average collection period measures the time it takes to convert receivables into cash. The ACP is influenced partly by economic conditions and partly by a set of controllable factors, termed *internal (management) factors*. Internal factors include credit policy variables (liberal, balanced, or conservative credit policy), credit terms, sales discounts, and collection.

Be cautious if you notice large inventory increases during periods of flat sales. Beware of the following inventory traps:

- Slow inventory turnover
- Faddish inventory
- Collateralized inventory
- Unjustified inventory shifts (such as changing from last in, first out [LIFO] to first in, first out [FIFO])
- Insufficient insurance
- Changes in divisional inventory valuation methods
- Increases in the number of LIFO pools
- Unreasonable intercompany profits
- Inclusion of inflationary profits in inventory
- Dangerous inventory increases brought on by attempts to hit a new product home run in a rundown stadium
- Gross profit trends weakening but no inventory markdowns in sight
- The presence of improper inventory charges: unjustified capitalized costs

You may want to ask your accountant to use receivables and inventory-related ratios to calculate cash increases or decreases rooted in fiscal receivables and inventory. The difference between "should have had" receivables and receivables that actually appeared on the latest fiscal statement denotes missing or lost cash flow creditors may be required to replace. Thus, if the purpose of a loan facility was originally planned to finance investment programs, do not be surprised if dialogue shifts to "you're asking us to finance stale current assets, not investments!" The *pro forma operating cash needs ratio – cash flow* derivation appears in Exhibit 6.3.

Operating Cash Sources

The term *operating cash sources* refers to operating current liabilities, including accounts payable and accruals. Short-term debt, the current portion of long-term debt, and commercial paper are not part of the mix. Watch for "bulges" in payables, which your lender may interpret as past-due payments to suppliers – and surely will if gross operating cash flow fails to contribute enough cash to help finance investment activities.

```
OPERATING CASH NEEDS ANALYSIS
Analysis of receivables
Accounts receivable 2013           –           55,886
Accounts receivable 2014           –           88,571
Sales 2013                         –          553,675
Sales 2014                         –          586,895
Average collection period 2013     –               37
Average collection period 2014     –               55

Substitute 2013 ACP; Solve Pro forma
Accounts receivable 2014 pro forma = 37*586,895/365
Accounts receivable 2014 pro forma         –   59,239
Accounts receivable 2014 actual            –   88,571
Excess accounts receivables         ⇨      –   29,332
DRAIN ON Net Cash Flow from Operations
```

```
Analysis of Inventory
Inventory 2013                                 99,087
Inventory 2014                                139,976
Cost of sales 2013                            450,394
Cost of sales 2014                            499,928
Inventory turnover 2013                          4.55
Inventory turnover 2014                          3.57

Substitute 2013 turnover; solve for inventory pro forma
Inventory pro forma 2014 = 499,928/4.56       109,985
Inventory 2014                                139,976
Excess inventory                     ⇨         29,991
Or, inventory that failed to convert to receivables
```

Exhibit 6.3. Operating Cash Needs Analysis

Net Cash Provided by Operating Activities

Theorem A – *Net Cash from Operating Activities:* If, on a sustainable basis, net cash flow from operations covers nondiscretionary investment activities, then finance activities are discretionary tempered at a very high probability. Discretionary financing activities lower asset and capital structure volatility along with credit risk.

Theorem B – *Net Cash from Operating Activities:* If, on a sustainable basis, net cash flow from operations falls far short of covering nondiscretionary investment, most firms will be forced to borrow. The capital structure tends to be less stable, and financial leverage increases along with default probabilities.

Net cash provided by operating activities is the central analytic theme, the line that reveals cash available to support investment activities after working capital has been covered by internal cash flow (gross operating cash flow plus operating cash needs net of operating cash sources). Working capital requirements can pull large amounts of cash from the business. Cash drains cut into capital expansion programs, especially if operating cash flow falls ominously below expectations. Keep in mind that one of the best ways to confirm earnings quality is to compare net income to net cash flow from operations. A case in point: if earnings consistently climb to high levels but little of the earnings turns to gross operating cash flow and liquidity (working capital) coverage, there will be hardly enough dollars to take care of investments or pay down debt. Cash flow, not profits, pays debt.

Investing Activities

Investing activities include advances and repayments to subsidiaries, securities transactions, and investments in long-term revenue-producing assets. Cash inflows from investment activities include proceeds from fixed asset disposals and proceeds from the sale of investment securities (Figure 6.2). Cash outflows include capital expenditures and stock purchases of other entities, project financing, capital and operating leases, and master limited partnerships.

Cash flows tied to property, plant, and equipment include fixed assets purchased through acquisitions and equipment purchases, capital leases, and proceeds from property disposals. Noncash transactions include translation gains and losses, transfers, depreciation, reverse consolidations, and restatements. Lenders do not usually require borrowers to break out property or equipment expenditures into maintenance of existing capacity or expenditures for expansion into new capacity, though this would be an ideal disclosure, since maintenance and capital expenditures are nondiscretionary outlays.

Companies with volatile cash flow histories tend to invest less on average than firms with smoother cash flows. They may also face stiffer costs when seeking funds from external capital markets. For firms with volatile cash flow patterns, business decisions are complicated by a greater tendency to incur periods of low internal cash flows that distract managers and cause them to throw out budgets, delay debt repayments, and defer capital expenditures.

We can categorize investment activities into two groups: discretionary and nondiscretionary.

Investment Activities		
Purchase of equipment	(300,000)	–
Decrease in notes receivable	15,000	–
Disposals	11,000	–
Total investment activities	–	(274,000)

Nondiscretionary investment activities refer to outlays required to keep a healthy and sustainable gross margin on the operating-unit level. Say, for example, your lender decides that nondiscretionary investments were covered fully by internal cash flow. From this premise they should assume financing activities were discretionary and your firm has adequate control of its capital structure. Assets require replacement or upgrading if operations are to be efficient. Depreciation expenses that consistently exceed capital expenditures are an indication of a declining, more expensive, less efficient operation. Watch out for outdated equipment and technology, high maintenance and repair expenses, a declining output level, inadequate depreciation charges, changes in depreciation methods, a lengthening depreciation period, a decline in the depreciation expense, and a large write-off of assets. Also be ready to explain distortions regarding currency translations. Check to see if deferred taxes are running off. Deferred taxes usually increase when capital expenditures accelerate. Download the most recent capital budgeting schedule.

Focus on project cost, net present values (NPVs), and internal rates of return (IRR). Check to see if fixed asset turnover (sales/net fixed assets) increases sharply. This ratio measures the turnover of plant and equipment in relation to sales. The fixed asset/turnover ratio is really a measure of cash flow efficiency, since it indicates how well fixed assets are being utilized. Determine if backlogs are increasing without a large pickup in sales. Unresolved backlogs usually happen only once, and then customers go elsewhere. Determine if work-in-progress inventory ties into weakened inventory turnover. Check to see if the gross margin trended down over the past few years due to increased labor costs and decreased operating leverage. If so, have a good explanation ready for your lender. Utilize real options tools when applicable.

Finally, consider your ownership position as far as unconsolidated investments are concerned. Cash inflows/outflows include dividends, advances, repayments, and stock acquisitions and sales. Noncash events include equity earnings and translation gains and losses. At your loan or investment interview, regard unconsolidated equity investments as a "don't ask, don't tell" affair. Lenders do not take it kindly when borrowers downstream funds to other businesses, particularly if loans were approved to support the original borrower's inventory, receivables, and value creating investments – not someone else's.

Financing Activities

This section of the statement of cash flows measures the flow of cash between creditors and obligors. Cash from financing activities includes new equity infusions, Treasury stock purchases and sales, and funded debt such as bonds, mortgages, notes, commercial paper, and short-term loans. Cash outflows consist of dividends, Treasury stock purchases, and loan payments.

Financing Activities		
Increase in long-term notes payable	378,000	–
Increase in short-term debt	72,000	–
New equity	20,000	–
Total financing activities	–	470,000

Positive numbers disclose cash flowing to your company. A negative result indicates the company has paid down debt or made dividend payments. Savvy business owners think in terms of optimal financing. Optimal financing is recognized as financing that minimizes cost of capital, maximizes equity value, and improves credit scores (or at least retards or prevent deteriorating credit scores). Analytics include matching decreases in long-term debt with increases in long-term debt, and in turn comparing these increases/decreases to gross operating cash flow (remember cash flow magnitude). For example, increases in long-term debt in an expanding business may exceed debt reductions. As long as debt-to-equity leverage along with other financial leverage ratios fall within acceptable ballpark levels, a lender will almost surely note that its customer's business contributes its fair share to financing activities.

We learn how to forecast our banker's cash flow in Chapter 7. We forecast financing requirements taking into account projected operating cash needs, sources, projected gross operating cash flow, projected revenue, change in revenue, projected operating current liabilities to revenue ratio, dividend payout rate, scheduled debt maturities, projected change in net fixed assets, and projected change in other assets.

CONCLUSION

Those of us who have studied cash flow and cash flow analysis no doubt understand the correlation between the flow of numbers and probabilities that loans will not be repaid. To those readers new to cash flow, I hope this chapter has shown that the whole is much more the sum of parts, the parts being an array of numbers, and the whole, enlightened credit judgment. Consider that at any given concert of Beethoven's *Eroica*, the power and intensity of the music will visibly shake people. If, at the concert's conclusion, you stroll by the orchestra pit and peek at the sheet music, you will likely think the score of this most towering work is a jumble of scribbles and scrawls. But to a musician, the scribbles come alive and resonate both in mind and soul. A musician actually hears Beethoven's rich organic sounds by simply looking at the score. Bars, clefs, keys, sharps, and flats are more than a short collection of scrawls on paper.

Like the *Eroica* score, a well-crafted cash flow and analysis is much more than a collection of bars, clefs, and keys. Rather, like many a great work, cash flow realizes subtle interactions beyond the obvious. Beautiful mathematics is, indeed, much like an elegant movement in a symphony.

CHAPTER 7

Interactive Business Forecasts Equations

OUTLINE

Cash flow projections help companies plan for the future. Projections involve predicting the outcome of alternative business strategies, including the future of the business as a whole, success of an existing or proposed product line, and industry prospects. For example, projections might focus on near-term profits, demand for products, and services, production costs, financial needs, and timing of loan repayments. Cash flow forecasting enables management to change strategies at the proper time to

Navigating the Business Loan. http://dx.doi.org/10.1016/B978-0-12-801698-5.00013-3

maximize goals or to avert losses. This is especially true of companies whose management operates with solid knowledge of their firm's nerve center: cash flow quality, magnitude, and trend.

The central issue in risk management deals with analyzing what could go wrong with individual credits and portfolios, and factoring this information into the analysis of risk-adjusted returns, capital adequacy, and loan provisions. "What if" analysis can unveil previously uncovered areas of credit risk exposure and plays the vital role of delving into areas of potential problems. Although a wide-ranging repertoire of projection analytics are in play when it comes to new product decision making, decisions to market new drugs, or streamlining corporate strategy, we will confine our study to creditor/client cash flow forecasting.

Creditors and potential investors take your business projections quite seriously. The Basel Committee on Banking Supervision has this to say about forecasting: "*In the final analysis banks should attempt to identify the types of situations, such as economic downturns, both in the whole economy or in particular sectors, higher than expected levels of delinquencies and defaults, or the combinations of credit and market events, that could produce substantial losses or liquidity problems. Stress test analyses should also include contingency plans regarding actions management might take given certain scenarios.*" [1]

The emphasis on bank forecasts developed as loan demand increased to fund large and complex credits including mergers and acquisitions. These new deals represented a new class of borrowers who pushed their financial structure to exceedingly high debt levels. As a result, lenders began to work with a new breed of sophisticated forecasting and valuation models to predict expected default, financial needs, and shareholder value with a great deal more accuracy and insight. Building projected financial statements around a set of critical assumptions or value drivers calls for research, logic, broad knowledge of a business and industry, and up-to-date predictive software.

Projections are essential tools because they offer precision, never accuracy. Nobody knows the future. Computers, after all, do not make

---

[1] Principles for the Management of Credit Risk, Basel Committee on Banking Supervision, Basel, September 2000, Principle 13.

credit decisions. They merely quantify assumptions about the future, serving as an additional analytic tool, albeit an important one, in the process of loan decision making. The real value of software is that technology facilitates rapid analysis of many alternatives, mimicking a realistic environment as much as possible. Sometimes, when appropriate, the bank will run a sensitivity analysis, examining the effect of changing key assumptions in any number of combinations to construct a range of outcomes from pessimistic to optimistic.

To determine the most suitable forecasting technique for a given situation, one of the first checks is comparability between forecast methods used and the complexity of data, or, for that matter, the deal itself. Experienced lenders are aware of both the benefits and pitfalls of each forecasting method before choosing one. It is not uncommon for a preferred forecasting method under certain conditions to offer incomplete, inaccurate results in one situation while producing acceptable results in another, similar analysis.

Availability of comprehensive, historical data is the standard prerequisite for developing forecasts. Since different forecasting methods generally require various amounts of historical data, requirements for data quality (and quantity) may vary as well. A few words on precision choices: a midsized triple-A operating in a nonvacillating environment and that submitted first-rate financial statements requires less forecasting data (because precision is less of an issue) than a B-rated borrower with observable risks.

SENSITIVITY FORECASTING: THE PERCENTAGE OF SALES METHOD

Do Financial Statements Make Sense?
Since balance sheet changes follow the income statement, the income statement is a logical point of departure. Balance sheets for internally generated sources of cash (payables, accruals, retained earnings, and other sources) depend on revenue and margin assumptions. Assets, uses of cash, are also tied to the income statement. A good test of income statement credibility is the comparison of pure output variables (POVs) with historical levels of projected pretax margins, after-tax margins, and the return on total assets. Sensitivity forecasts are time-tested, efficient

methods to advance strategic plans, and with today's technology, can easily be entered into a financial calculator. You can put your accounting hat away! You will gain more perception, precision, and knowledge of your firm's strategic planning process and financing requirements by pressing a few keys on your cell phone than you would by analyzing a full set of projected statements.

Sensitivity forecasting involves two formulas, the F and the E equations. Forecast results processed by the two equations yield the same outcome as projected full financials.

Our Plan
1. Introduce and quickly review F and E equations.
2. Open the short case Zarch, Inc.
3. Check adjustments to key forecast ratios (we reviewed ratios in Chapter 4, Ratios Every Business Should Monitor); we will put your cash flow expertise to work.
4. Enter Zarch key forecast in the F and E formulas.
5. Verify that the two equations' outcomes are identical to Zarch, Inc. projected financial statements.
6. Install the following app in your cell or tablet: 17BII+ Financial Calculator by R.L.M. Software. This app is available from Google Play for Android or the App Store for iTunes.
7. Enter F, E, F*, and sustainable growth equations into your cell or tablet's 17BII + financial calculator's SOLVER. Once done, there are no formulas to worry about or financial statements to review. Simply press keys on your cell or tablet and observe the following:
   a. Amount of external financing required over the forecast horizon
   b. Percentage of sales increases calling for external financing
   c. Sales growth rate in equilibrium with your firm's financial structure
   d. Changes to your financial plan limiting debt to an amount that will not put a strain on financial leverage
   e. Percentage of sales increase capable of being financed internally
   f. Gross operating cash flow needed to help finance a firm internally.

INTRODUCTION TO THE F AND E EQUATIONS

F = cumulative financial needs
A = projected assets
S = projected sales
ΔS = change in sales
L1 = projected operating current liabilities (e.g., accounts payable and accruals)
P = projected profit margin (%)
d = dividend payout rate
R = debt maturities
G or g = sales growth rate

Equation One: F Equation

The F equation determines your firm's external financing over a discrete forecast horizon.

$$F = A/S\,(\Delta S) - L1/S\,(\Delta S) - P(S)(1 - d) + R$$

Equation Two: E Equation

The E equation determines how much sales growth requires external financing over a discrete forecast horizon.

$$E = (A/S - L_1/S) - (P/g)(1 + g)(1 - d) + R/(\Delta S)$$

If E reaches 95% in the projection period, only 5% of sales growth will be internally financed – an immediate storm signal, if your lender informed you that last year's financial leverage was excessive.

Setting E to zero and solving for g, your sales growth rate, will give you a fast reading on the quality and magnitude of future cash flows. Say E is set to zero while g falls somewhere in the first industry quartile. This result means your firm's sales level, among the best in the industry, can be financed with internal cash flow – no debt needed. Here is another example. Let us assume that base-year leverage is high and you want to reduce leverage by ensuring internal financing levels are set at 40%. Set the equation at 60% and solve for the capital output ratio (assets/sales) required to make your strategy work. If embedded ratios (receivables, inventory, and fixed assets) are below industry or benchmarks, call a meeting of the department heads and read them the riot act.

Since balance sheet changes are correlated to some extent with your firm's income statement, the income statement is a logical point of departure. Internally generated sources of cash (payables, accruals, retained earnings, and other sources) are influenced by revenue and net margin assumptions. Assets, uses of cash, are also tied to the income statement. A good test of income statement credibility is the historical comparison of forecast ratios and other variables: projected pretax margins, after-tax margins, the return on total assets, and other variables.

17BII+ Financial Calculator App Case

Consider the historical financial statements of Zarch, Inc. for the fiscal period ending December 31, 2013. This young growth company is a producer of cable for the computer industry and is requesting a $50 million loan for plant expansion. The expansion program is needed to raise operating leverage, reduce labor costs, improve production efficiency, and increase the gross profit margin. Management presented the following historical and projected financial statements to their bankers in support of their request for a loan.

Zarch, Inc.
Historical Balance Sheet
12/31/13
(In Thousands)

	Percent of Sales	
Cash	2,000	.02
Accounts Receivable	4,000	.04
Inventories	54,000	.54
Plant and Equipment	60,000	.60
Total Assets	120,000	1.20
Accounts Payable	20,000	.20
Accruals	6,000	.06
Long-term Debt	44,000	Constant **
Capital Stock	10,000	Constant **
Paid In Capital	10,000	Constant **
Retained Earnings	30,000	Earnings Retention
Total liabilities and equity	120,000	

** Financing decision; does not vary with sales

Exhibit 7.1. Zarch, Inc. Historical financial statements.

Zarch Inc.
Historical Income Statement
12/31/13
(In Thousands)

		Percent of Sales
Net Sales	100,000	1.00
Cost of Goods Sold	75,000	.75
Gross margin	25,000	.25
Expenses	23,000	.23
Net Income	2,000	.02

Projected Fiscal 2014 Sales 150,000

Exhibit 7.1. (Continued)

		Percent of Sales
Cash	3,000	.02
Accounts Receivable	6,000	.04
Inventories	81,000	.54
Net Plant and Equipment	90,000	.60
Total Assets	180,000	1.20
Accounts Payable	30,000	.20
Accruals	9,000	.06
Long-term Debt	44,000	Constant
Capital Stock	10,000	Constant
Paid In Capital	10,000	Constant
Retained Earnings	33,000*	Earnings Retention
Available Capitalization	136,000	
Financial Needs	**44,000**	**Derived**
Total Liabilities and Equity 180,000		

* $30,000 + .02($150,000) – 0 = $33,000

Exhibit 7.2. Zarch, Inc. Projected financial statements, December 31, 2014.

F Equation Results

Open the **SOLVER** and press SOLVE/NEW. In the yellow box enter F equation exactly as it appears below. Use the ( ) keys, divide key ÷ multiplication key ×, and plus/minus keys that appears on the app, not from your device. Within the equations & replaces Δ. Be sure to SAVE

F = A/S×&S − L1/S×&S − P×S×(1 − D). Press DONE/ADD. The F equation now appears in the yellow screen.

Press CALC. If you entered the formula correctly, variables appear as blue keys.

Financial Needs Input and Solutions

F Equation Variables	What Variable Means	Value	10BII Financial Calculator
A/S	Capital output ratio	180,000/150,000 = 1.2	Enter 1.2 in the A/S blue key
&S	Change in sales	50,000	Enter 50,000 in &S blue key
S	Projected sales	150,000	Enter 150,000 in the S blue key
L1/S	Spontaneous liabilities/sales	(30,000 + 9,000)/ 150,000 = .26	Enter .26 into L1/S blue key
P	Projected profit margin (%)	.02	Enter .02 in the P blue key
D	Dividend payout rate	0	Enter 0 in the D blue key
F	Projected financial needs	Dependent variable We solve for F	Press the F key; F = 44,000. Compare this number to financial needs appearing on the projected balance sheet. Verify that the two numbers are identical.

F Equation Point at Issue	Approach	Solution	Implication
How much financing will my firm require in 2014?	–	44,000	–
The firm's financial leverage is high. The bank wants to limit financing to 29,000. What should I do?	Increase profit margin	Select the F equation to open. Tap CALC. Enter 29,000 F; 150,000 S; .29 L1/S; 50,000 &S. Solve for P. P = .21, the profit margin in equilibrium with limited financing.	Zarch, Inc. requires a 21% profit margin to offset the lower amount the bank is willing to lend.
Same as above	Reduce the capital output ratio, assets/sales, and make assets more efficient	Clear data. Enter 29,000 F; 150,000 S; L1/S .29; 50,000 &S; .02 P. Solve for A/S. A/S = .93	In order for the firm to carry less debt, the capital output ratio must be reduced from 1.2 to .93. Since the ratio is made of the average collection period, inventory turnover, and fixed asset turnover, you may need to either collect receivables faster to improve inventory management or reduce fixed assets with some outsourcing.

Percentage of Sale Increase Requiring Outside Financing: Equation Input and Solutions

Open the SOLVER and press SOLVE/NEW. In the yellow box enter E equation exactly as it appears below. Be sure to SAVE.

$$E = A/S - L1/S) - (P \div G \times (1 + G) \times (1 - D))$$

The E formula identifies the percentage of sales growth requiring external financing. The two equations are interconnected since they both are derived from the popular IAS and FAS cash flow statement.

For example, firms with high growth potential create shareholder value. That aphorism is as old as the hills, yet a high-growth firm running on high-octane fixed assets can push the firm to the brink.

E Equation Variable	What Variable Means	Value	10BII Financial Calculator
A/S	Capital output ratio	Projected assets/projected sales = 180,000/150,000 = 1.2	Enter 1.2 in the A/S key
P	Projected profit margin (%)	.02	Enter .02 in the P key
G	Sales growth rate	(150,000–100,000)/ 100,000 = .5	Enter .5 in the G key
D	Dividend payout rate	0	Enter 0 in the D key
E	Percent of sales increase that must be externally financed = dependent variable we solve for	Solve for E by pressing the blue key. E = .88 Y	88% of sales growth must be externally financed, with 22% financed by internal cash flow. This will place additional strain on the capital structure by increasing the debt/equity ratio (leverage).

Formula Validation

The firm's projected sales growth is set at 50,000. Thus .88 (50,000) = 44,000, the same amount identified in the F equation and the financial needs line in financial projections.

E Equation Concerns	Approach	Solution	Implication
My bank will not finance more than 60% of my sales growth. What do I need to do to finance the rest?	Try reducing assets, making them more efficient.	Clear data; load the E equation. Tap CALC. Enter .6 E; .29 L1/S; .5 G; 0 D; 50,000 &S. Solve for A/S. A/S = .93	In order to reduce the capital/output ratio to a more efficient 93% from 120%, receivables, inventory, or fixed assets must be lowered in order to increase internal financing capacity. Remember, asset reductions are cash sources.
What sales growth rate is the firm capable of financing internally?	Set E at zero and solve for G.	Clear data; load the E equation. Tap CALC. Enter 0 E; .29 L1/S; .02 P; 0 D; Solve for G by tapping the blue G key. G = .02	The firm is capable of sustaining a 2% sales growth rate financed internally. This will require management to reassess all the variables included in the calculation to determine how projections can be supported with only internal funds. Based on the examples discussed above for the F equation, managers can manipulate assets, liabilities, sales, profits, dividends, and the growth rate to determine if this exercise is feasible. If nothing else is accomplished, financial management will better understand the company's true status and how changes made in management policy can improve the business.

Equation Three: F* Equation: The Bankers Cash Flow Forecast Equation

This equation is tailored for lenders and advanced users. I encourage you to review Chapter 6. Recall that our banker's cash flow statement separates cash and cash equivalents into operating, investing, and financial activities. Further refinements deal with operating current asset and operating current liabilities, given as operating cash needs and operating cash sources. Projected operating cash need is equal to A1/S times ΔS whereas projected operating cash sources equal L1/S times ΔS. Forecast changes in net fixed assets arise from adjustments to prior period net fixed asset reconciliations.

F* = projected financing activities to be determined
A1/S = projected operating current assets to sales or revenue ratio = .66
GOCF = projected gross operating cash flow = 3,900,000
S = projected sales = 24,500,000
ΔS = change in sales or revenue = 1,126,500
L1/S = projected operating current liabilities to sales ratio
(e.g., accounts payable and accruals) = .35
D = projected dividend payout rate = .25
R = scheduled debt maturities = 1,500,000
ΔNFA = projected change in net fixed assets = 4,300,000
ΔOA = projected change in other assets = 2,500,000

$$F* = (A1/S \times \&S + \&NFA + \&OA) - L1/S \times \&S - (GOCF \div S \times S \times (1 - D)) + R.$$

Press DONE/ADD. The F equation now appears in the yellow screen.

F* Projected Cash Flow Financing Activities = 5,724,215

Assume the bank limits loan facilities to 4,000,000 and wants the firm to employ more efficient operating current asset policies and reduce its dividend payout rate. What gross operating cash flow will be required to partially offset the reduced loan facility, restrictions on operating current assets, and dividend policy?

1. The obligor agrees to cut inventory, launching "just in time" inventory policies. As a result, operating current assets to sales ratio, A1/S reduces to .40 from .66.
2. Dividend payout decreases to .05 from .25.

Enter 40,00,000 F*, .05 D, .66, A 1/S .40. Tap GOCF. GOCF = 4,585,606.

The projected financing plan is both reasonable and attainable given gross operating cash flow last period was 3,900,000.

The Sustainable Growth Model: A Forecasting Tool Especially Tailored to Thinly Capitalized, Rapid-Growth Firms

Small businesses can get into trouble if they grow too fast. Will they be able to sustain an upsurge in orders, fulfill expanding production demand, hire and train enough qualified people, and attract financing to satisfy higher cash needs? Rapid-growth firms can stream negative operating cash flows for years before becoming cash producers. The higher the rate of spending, the greater the possibilities of being forced to seek additional funding. If funding becomes unavailable, trouble may be just around the corner. Eventually, the majority of fast-growth companies become slow-growth companies. Some managers fail to see the writing on the wall and pursue growth long after expansion opportunities have passed. In these cases, there is a real possibility of destabilizing the capital structure, to the dismay of lenders and investors. If you are a growing business or have dreams of becoming one, you need to convince lenders and investors that you are not only mindful of the risks of growth, but also that your business plan and demographic analysis are properly hedged against uncertainty and are on solid ground.

Many financing sources, including venture capitalists, receive more than 5,000 business plans per year, all competing against your business plan for funding consideration. Only 10% of these plans are seriously considered, and 1–2% are actually funded. In this section, we will work numbers, integrate growth stresses and offsetting strategies in business plan format, and try to get you to the front of the line.

Sustainable growth analysis is remarkably suited for this type of analysis because it deals with the possibilities that revenue increases of highly leveraged growth companies put stress on the financial structure. Marvelous ideas and outstanding revenue/profit predictions are centerpieces of many investment-procuring slide shows, but unless you convince investors that your business plan is all about sustainability management, that your firm is sound now, and that it will continue to be when trouble hits (as it inevitably will), be prepared to move to the back of the funding line.

Sustainable growth methodology helps to identify the proportion of growth fueled through internal versus external cash flow. Results are set against different degrees of tolerance by manipulating specific variables to determine various levels of risk. Thus, sustainable growth acts as a barometer, checking whether or not revenue growth rates are in equilibrium with a firm's capital structure. In other words, is the firm growing too fast for its own good?

Within the model's core is the sustainable growth rate, the maximum revenue growth rate (over the foreseeable future) realizable without putting stress on a balance sheet. In simple terms, firms need money to make money, but must also aim to strike an optimal balance between debt and equity. If the relationship between liabilities and net worth deteriorates, lenders and investors are bound to question management's competence and will usually stay clear of financing requests.

Consider the historical financial statements of Landon, Inc. for the fiscal period ending December 31, 2014. The company operates as a producer of printing press rollers. Management wants to expand operations into innovative 3-D printing. The firm recently exhausted its debt capacity and is having trouble finding cash to set up the promising new business. Management has asked an angel investment group if they would be willing to take a $50 million equity position to finance the purchase of large scale equipment and manufacturing facilities.

What are the angel investors' major concerns? In their business plans, management frequently presents projected growth in annual revenues and profits. The fast growth rate looks impressive on the surface, but the lack of restraint leaves the opposite impression with angel investors. The more exaggerated the story, the more investors question management's business judgment. These investors look for business strategies that make practical sense and understand the risks of creating and marketing new technology; they want assurance that the balance sheet will not collapse at the first sign of trouble.

Management presented historical and projected financial statements to the angel investors. Pertinent information was extracted, including net profit margin, dividend payout rate, capital output (assets to sales), and targeted growth rates. Projections included the plant expansion program associated with the firm's funding requirements. Results are summarized below.

Profit Margin	Dividend Payout	Capital Output	Limit Placed on Financial Leverage by Angel Investors	Targeted Growth Rate
7.0%	60.0%	180.0%	150.0%	10.0%

The investor group used the sustainable growth equation in order to be reasonably sure the firm could expand operations prudently and not end up as just one more failed business.

Equation Four: The Sustainable Growth Model

The sustainable growth rate, $g*$, is the maximum growth rate in sales (over the foreseeable future) that a firm can achieve without placing excessive strain on its financial structure. In simple terms, operations need money to make money. Sustainable growth solutions deal with boosting equity when volume accelerates. The objective: maintaining the right balance between liabilities and equity. Industry benchmarks act as points of reference and reflect the cumulative decisions of management, lenders, suppliers, customers, and competitors. Whenever the relationship between liabilities and net worth is significantly beyond industry standards, questions arise about management's competence and the firm's unsystematic risk control.

$$g* = \frac{P\,(1-D)\,(1+L)}{A/S - P\,(1-D)\,(1+L)}$$

A/S = projected capital output ratio (assets/sales)
L = debt to equity ratio limit placed by lenders or investors
$g*$ = sustainable growth rate
P = projected profit margin (%)
D = dividend payout rate
T = targeted sales growth rate (applies to the sustainable growth formula)

Open SOLVER and press SOLVE/NEW. In the yellow box enter the $g*$ sustainable growth equation exactly as it appears below. Be sure to SAVE as Sustainable Growth Model.

$$g* = (P \times (1-D) \times (1+L)) \div (A/SP \times (1-D) \times (1+L))$$

Press DONE/ADD. The g* equation now appears in the yellow screen.

Press CALC. If you entered the formula correctly, variables appear as blue keys on your cell phone or tablet.

Sustainable Growth Equation Variable	What Variable Means	Value	10BII Financial Calculator Entry
g*	Sustainable growth rate	Dependent variable we solve for	Tap g*
A/S	Capital output ratio, that is, projected assets/projected sales	1.8	Enter 1.8 in the A/S key
P	Projected profit margin (%)	.07	Enter .07 in the P key
L	Financial leverage (debt to equity ratio) ceiling set by the angel investors. Landon has maxed out bank facilities and is currently stretched to the limit. The group was certain that financial leverage above the set ceiling would trigger financial distress.	1.50	Enter 1.5 in the L key
D	Dividend payout rate	.60	Enter .6 in the D key

Solve for g*, the sustainable growth rate, by tapping the g* key. The sustainable growth rate, g*, is 4% versus the 10% targeted sales growth rate. Investors watch out! The sustainable growth model indicates that the firm can sustain a 4% revenue growth rate over the foreseeable future without raising financial leverage beyond the ceiling set by angel investors. However, Landon is expected to grow at a 10% rate, not a 4% rate, which will cause financial leverage to exceed the maximum (150%) set by the investment group.

Next, the investment group set g* equal to the targeted growth rate and solved for L (now a dependent variable) in order to uncover the financial leverage in equilibrium with the firm's targeted growth rate. The concern is: if the firm continues its growth pattern, how high will leverage climb, assuming the firm raises no new equity?

Let us try this operation. Enter .10, the targeted growth rate, in place of g* and tap the L key. L = 484%. The result shows that financial leverage must increase to 484% for sales growth and the financial structure to join in equilibrium, a percentage well beyond limits insisted upon by angel investors. This wise and conservative group unequivocally demanded that revenue growth rate be linked to the firm's financial structure to preserve under-risk balance sheet integrity – hardly possible with potential leverage pegged at 484% and debt capacity at the present time close to zero.

The proposal is too risky and not about to close. Had the firm consented to match angel cash infusions with additional owner equity, improve capital output by means of outsourcing, hold dividends in check, or offered to liquidate unprofitable assets, the negotiations would have moved forward.

Let us see if things might have worked out differently. The capital output ratio is excessive but could be reduced significantly if management contracts out production to outsourcers. Fixed assets, raw materials, and work-in-process inventory contracts, admittedly not a sweet pill to swallow since the final product will cost more to produce. Secondly, dividends must be lowered or eliminated. Dividends are a double-edged sword: dividends take from cash flow, and also lower equity. How could this deal have moved forward if management agreed to lower capital output and dividends? See the table below.

	Profit Margin	Dividend Payout	Capital Output	Limit Placed on Financial Leverage	Targeted Growth Rate
Original plan	7.0%	60.0%	180.0%	150.0%	10.0%
Revised plan	4.0% (subcontracting production and marketing will increase cost of goods sold)	10.0%	90% (outsourcing will reduce fixed assets and inventory)	150.0%	10.0%

Enter .04 P; .1 D; .9 A. Tap g*. g* = .11. The new sustainable rate is 11%, meaning the firm can increase revenue at the rate of 11% annually without pushing leverage beyond the 150% limit set by the investment group. However, the targeted growth rate is only 10%, which means financial leverage is likely to fall below 150%. These very smart investors realized early on that problems stemmed from the firm's overheated balance sheet, not its operating statement. There is a lesson to be learned here. Pitching for investment money is a science as well as an art, so do not exaggerate sales and profits. Few will be impressed. Instead, focus on balance sheet sustainability and the firm's ability to shift gears if things go wrong.

A SIMULATIONS APPROACH TO FINANCIAL FORECASTING

Standard forecasting models rely on single sets of assumptions, which usually lead to two outcomes: base case and worst. But static forecasting (base and worse cases) limits the variability of outcomes. It is difficult to know which of a series of strategic options the borrower will pursue without analyzing differences in both the range and distribution shape of possible outcomes and the most likely result associated with each option. A simulation is a computer-assisted extension of sensitivity forecasting (as an add-on to your computer workbook). Simulations help answer questions like:

- "Will the borrower stay under budget if the bank finances the facility?"
- "What are the chances the project will finish on time and in the money?"
- "What are the probabilities that operating cash flow will cover debt service when all is said and done?"
- "Is multicollinearity a problem with the forecast?"

Introducing the technique known as Monte Carlo simulation, an entire range of results and confidence levels is feasible for any given forecast run. The principle behind Monte Carlo simulation is its ability to conceptualize real-world situations involving elements of uncertainty too complex to be solved with less sophisticated methods. It is a technique requiring a random number generator set in the program. Real Options Valuation, @Risk, and Crystal Ball are three popular programs that generate random numbers for assumption cells you define. Using these random numbers, simulation programs compute the formulas in the forecast cells. This is a continuous process that recalculates each forecast formula over and over again. Developing a simulation is not difficult.

Visit the Real Options Valuation website: http://www.realoptions valuation.com/

1. Click Downloads/White Papers and Downloads/A Quick Primer on Risk and Decision Analysis for Everyone: Applying Monte Carlo Simulation, Real Options, Forecasting, and Portfolio Optimization.

2. Click Downloads/Getting Started and Modeling Videos/Video A: Risk Simulator: Quick Getting Started Guide (13 min). This is a quick high-level overview video that very briefly introduces the various Risk Simulator modules

3. Click Downloads/Sample Models/Basic Simulation Model

CHAPTER 8

Assets You Can Pledge to Support Your Business Loan*

OUTLINE

*Please visit http://booksite.elsevier.com/9780128016985 to view the ancillary material of this chapter.

Navigating the Business Loan. http://dx.doi.org/10.1016/B978-0-12-801698-5.00007-8

ACCOUNTS RECEIVABLE, INVENTORY, PURCHASE ORDER FINANCING, AND FACTORING

Lenders take collateral to reduce the risks of some business loans, but most credit approvals are based on repayment capacity. Collateral should not act as a replacement for due diligence. Values may be impaired by the very factors that led to the diminished recoverability of the credit itself in the first place. Your lender works with policies and procedures governing suitability, value, and enforceability. Businesses not capable of unsecured borrowing generally find themselves in that position for the following reasons:

1. A business may be new and unproven
2. There may be some question concerning ability to service unsecured debt
3. Proposed financing requests may be too large to justify unsecured credit
4. Working capital and profits were insufficient to perform periodic cleanup of short-term advances
5. Working capital is inadequate for sales volume and type of operation
6. Previous unsecured borrowings are no longer warranted because unfavorable credit dynamics were linked to a business
7. The loan facility requested exceeded the unsecured credit limit

Asset-based financing offers several benefits to borrowers: it is an efficient way to finance expanding operations because borrowing capacity expands along with sales; it permits borrowers to take advantage of purchase discounts because cash is received immediately upon sales, thus permitting prompt payment to suppliers, which earns the company a reputation good enough to reduce the cost of purchases; and it ensures a revolving, expanding line of credit.

Secured loans make it possible for you and your business to repair a damaged credit score, because as long as you pay on time, lenders will file positive credit reports. Secured loans offer the opportunity to choose between fixed or variable rates, and you also have the choice to pay nothing for the initial term of the loan. This means greater financial flexibility and more savings options. If you think you will not be able to reduce loan balances in a timely manner, you can ask to extend terms.

On the flip side, asset-based lending offers certain advantages to the lender: collateral loans generate relatively high yields; asset-based lending results in depository relationships; it offers an ongoing relationship with long-standing customers whose financial condition no longer warrants unsecured credit; it generates new business; and it minimizes potential loss because loans are structured as formula-based facilities, whereby advances are made against a percentage of acceptable collateral.

A security interest arises when collateralized assets provide the lender rights to claim assets pledged before other creditors. If a borrower defaults and collateral is sold for less than the loan amount, the lender becomes a general or unsecured creditor for the balance. Secured loans require documentation generally known as security agreements. A lender's security interest in collateral is formalized with a security agreement signed by both lender and borrower, known as the parties, and filed with a public officer – usually the secretary of state – in the state in which the collateral is located. This filing gives public notice to interested parties that the lender has prior claim to the collateral. Before approving advances, lenders search public records to ensure pledged assets are not secured elsewhere.

The Uniform Commercial Code (UCC) deals with lender protection on security interests. Lenders should be familiar with the code before they obtain a security interest in collateral. Under Article 9 of the UCC, the lender must create a valid and enforceable security interest and "perfect" that interest. Once enforceable security interest is created, the secured party can always enforce it, on default, against the debtor, provided there is no superior third-party interest. If the holder of a valid and enforceable Article 9 interest takes the additional steps required under Article 9 to perfect the interest, it will defeat most such third parties. Sections 9-203 and 9-204 of the UCC require that the parties take four steps to create a valid and enforceable security interest:

- Enter into a security agreement
- Reduce as much of that agreement to writing as is necessary to satisfy Section 9-203 (which also requires that the debtor sign this writing), or as is necessary for the creditor to have possession of the collateral
- Have the debtor acquire rights in the collateral
- Have the secured party give value to the collateral

The Federal Reserve also provides guidelines concerning the collateral used to secure loans. The following questions from its Commercial Bank Examination Manual should be considered before entering into a security agreement[1]:

1. Is negotiable collateral held under joint custody?
2. Has the customer obtained and filed for released collateral and signed a receipt?
3. Are securities and commodities valued and margin requirements reviewed at least monthly?
4. When the support rests on the cash surrender value of insurance policies, is a periodic accounting received from the insurance company and maintained with the policy?
5. Is a record maintained of entry to the collateral vault?
6. Are stock powers filed separately to bar negotiability and to deter abstraction of both the security and the negotiating instrument?
7. Are securities out for transfer, exchange, and so on controlled by renumbered temporary vault out tickets?
8. Has the lender instituted a system that ensures that (1) security agreements are filed; (2) collateral mortgages are properly recorded; (3) title searches and property appraisals are performed in connection with collateral mortgages; and (4) insurance coverage (including loss payee clause) is in effect on property covered by collateral mortgages?

---

[1] Division of Banking Supervision and Regulation, Federal Reserve System, Commercial Bank Examination Manual, October 2009, Section 2160: Asset-Based Lending

9. Are acknowledgments received for pledged deposits held at other lenders?
10. Is an officer's approval necessary before collateral can be released or substituted?
11. Does the lender have an internal review system that re-examines collateral items for negotiability and proper assignment, checks values assigned to collateral when the loan is made and at frequent intervals thereafter, determines that items out on temporary vault out tickets are authorized and have not been outstanding for an unreasonable length of time, and determines that loan payments are promptly posted?
12. Are all notes assigned consecutive numbers and recorded on a note register or similar record? Do numbers on notes agree with those recorded on the register?
13. Are collection notices handled by someone not connected with loan processing?
14. In mortgage warehouse financing, does the lender hold the original mortgage note, trust deed, or other critical document, releasing only against payment?
15. Have standards been set for determining the percentage advance to be made against acceptable receivables?
16. Are acceptable receivables defined?
17. Has the lender established minimum requirements for verification of the borrower's accounts receivable and established minimum standards for documentation?
18. Have accounts receivable financing policies been reviewed at least annually to determine if they are compatible with changing market conditions?
19. Have loan statements, delinquent accounts, collection requests, and past due notices been checked with the trial balances that are used in reconciling subsidiary records of accounts receivable financing loans with general ledger accounts?
20. Have inquiries about accounts receivable financing loan balances been answered and investigated?
21. Is the lender in receipt of documents supporting recorded credit adjustments to loan accounts or accrued interest receivable accounts? Have these documents been checked or tested subsequently?

22. Are terms, dates, weights, description of merchandise, and so on shown on invoices, shipping documents, delivery receipts, and bills of lading? Are these documents scrutinized for differences?
23. Were payments from customers scrutinized for differences in invoice dates, numbers, terms, and so on?
24. Do lender records show, on a timely basis, a first lien on the assigned receivables for each borrower?
25. Do loans granted on the security of the receivables also have an assignment of the inventory?
26. Does the lender verify the borrower's accounts receivable or require independent verification on a periodic basis?
27. Does the lender require the borrower to provide aged accounts receivable schedules on a periodic basis?

ACCOUNTS RECEIVABLE FINANCING

Illustrative Example: Borrowing Base Facility

Location: Models are available on the Elsevier Website. http://www.elsevierdirect.com/companion

Brief description: Applies accounts receivable borrowing base analysis, auditing procedures, acceptance/rejection cost modeling, and cash budget analysis to the approval process.

Accounts receivables financing is an arrangement whereby a bank or finance company either advances funds by purchasing invoices or accounts receivables outright over time (factoring) or lends against receivables backed by an assignment on pledged receivables. Factoring is conducted on a notification basis (the client's customer is notified that the factor purchased receivables), whereas straight receivable financing is practiced on a nonnotification basis. Even if collateral quality is solid and in excess of advances, a borrower must still demonstrate it is a viable business. Collateral offered by a distressed borrower may face legal challenges if prior claims surface and it is known that advances were made with prior knowledge of the borrower's deteriorated condition. Receivables are usually pledged on a notification basis. Under this method, the lender maintains complete control of all funds paid on accounts pledged by requiring the borrower's customer to remit directly to a lock box.

Lenders take receivables that are current or not more than a given number of days past due. The entire amount of receivables may be unacceptable if a certain percentage (e.g., 10%) is 90 days or more delinquent. In addition, a limit is placed on the maximum dollar amount due from any one account debtor, since there is always the possibility of unforeseen and undisclosed credit failure or a return of merchandise. A common benchmark is to have no more than 20% of assigned receivables from one customer. To verify the authenticity of pledged collateral, lenders institute a program of direct confirmation. This procedure is particularly important if receivables are pledged on a nonnotification basis, since the lender does not have the same control of the debtor accounts as it does when the receivables are pledged on a notification basis.

The quality of pledged receivables depends on turnover ratios, monthly aging, concentration, eligibility, related parties, and additional measures, which are discussed in the following points:

1. Reduced turnover indicates reduced quality.
2. Monthly aging points to delinquencies as a percent of total accounts pledged, lower portfolio mix, and past due balances alongside current amounts due.
3. Concentration is associated with increased vulnerability to loss if a large percentage of assigned receivables is limited to a few accounts.
4. Ineligible receivables are excluded from the lending formula, such as those due from affiliated companies (while such receivables might be valid, the temptation to create fraudulent invoices would be great), and receivables subject to a purchase money interest, such as floor plan arrangements.

Formula-Based Loans

Formula-based loans are established on a borrowing base formula. The formula determines which assets will be loaned against, the minimum acceptable quality of those assets, and the amount of cushion required to reduce exposure risks. Losses are rare if there is more than enough strong collateral to cover outstanding loans. Newly created receivables feed into a pool, while reductions flow from payments on account, returns and allowances, bad debts, and the charges from seriously past-due accounts. Rates are quoted as a spread over the prime lending rate.

In addition to charging interest – at two or three percentage points above prime – it is customary to impose a service charge amounting to 1% or 2% of the borrower's average loan balance. Receivables accepted into a borrowing base arrangement usually have high marks when it comes to the credit standing of the borrower's customers, age and size of receivables, merchandise quality, number of returns due to missed season and/or faulty merchandise, the borrower's competitive position, funds generated in the account, and a borrower's customer credit policies.

Loan Agreement

Important items usually covered by a loan agreement for accounts receivable financing include the following:

1. Duration of the lending arrangement
2. Right of the lender to screen the accounts presented to it by the borrower to determine which are acceptable as security
3. Procedure by which accounts held by the lender are to be replaced or the loan reduced if they become past due
4. Percentage the lender will advance against the face amount of receivables
5. Maximum total advances
6. Reports indicating amounts owed by each customer
7. As additional sales are made, the borrower may be required to submit copies of invoices or other evidence of shipment
8. Responsibility of the borrower to forward directly to the lender payments received on assigned accounts
9. Authorization to inspect borrower's books and to verify accounts receivable through confirmation by a public accounting firm or other agency

Formula Certificate

Lenders require a loan formula certificate completed and signed by an official in the borrowing firm. The certificate includes total receivables and inventory, eligible receivables and inventory, loan amount outstanding, and the debt amount over or under allowed borrowings. Additional advances should be forthcoming if sufficient collateral is available. The debt is to be reduced if it is over the amount allowed as shown by the loan formula certificate. Except in special circumstances, advances are limited to 75% or 80% of eligible accounts receivable.

Ineligible receivables include accounts more than 90 days past due, those that are intercompany or from related businesses, and those that have offsetting payables or prepayments. To derive the exposure percentage, divide accounts receivable advances into net collateral. Net collateral represents assigned receivable plus blocked cash accounts, less dilution and 90 days past due receivables. Results are plotted against the borrower's records. While minor differences are ignored, ledger accounts may reveal major discrepancies, such as unreported receipts. Lender responsibilities follow designated policies and procedures to ensure the safety and integrity of assigned receivables. The affairs of the borrower, together with loan status, are policed on a regular basis. Advances against collateral must see to it that public filings are recorded properly and state statutes followed with regard to locale and number of filings needed to ensure a proper lien.

THE ACCOUNTS RECEIVABLE AUDIT: SCOPE AND DETAILS

To verify information, lenders may sometimes commission the audit to outside financing agents. Following is a step-by-step approach to auditing accounts receivable as a security:

Step 1: Financial Statements
Current information fundamental to a sound audit includes trial balances, interim statements, cash budgets, invoice copies, and ledger computer printouts.

Step 2: Receivables Overview
Auditors conduct a credit check on large positions. Three sources of credit information include agency reports, financial institutions, and suppliers. Ratings are evaluated, recorded, and classified as acceptable or unacceptable. Additional measures of receivable quality, or lack thereof, include collection period, proximity to economically depressed areas, diversification, and optimal composition of the receivables portfolio. Receivable concentrations are prudently watched. The danger of some firm controlling the obligor looms large, particularly if the

business deteriorated. For example, a borrower's customer may start dictating unfavorable credit terms or threaten to cancel orders at the slightest provocation. Key auditing points are the following:

1. Evaluate concentrated receivables methodically with regard to account classification and aging.
2. Credit reports and checkings obtained on the largest accounts include agency reports, lenders, trade journals, suppliers, and credit reporting agencies. Receivables are confirmed by contacting trade debtors, and the collection period for each account is computed.
3. Accounts are classified as acceptable or unacceptable.
4. Receivables quality measures are judged by collection period, delinquency ratio (past due receivables over credit sales), and bad debt ratio (write-offs over net receivables).
5. Files of past-due accounts are checked for recent correspondence and collection effort. Large positions are quizzed judiciously.

7.3.3 Step 3: Accounts Receivable Aging

	Amount ($)	Percent (%)
0–30	45,000	63.3
30–45	11,300	16.6
45–60	6,500	9.6
60–90	3,200	4.7
90 or more	1,900	2.8
Total	67,900	100.0

Aging of receivables logged as 0–30 days, 30–45 days, 45–60 days, and 60–90 days. Accounts 90 days or more past due are measured by dividing individual receivables into the total, as seen in Exhibit 7.1. Accounts over 90 days past due are frequently discarded. Concentration is tested by (1) acceptable receivables to total receivables, and (2) the average of the five largest receivables summed to total receivables. The average size of accounts is measured to determine expense allocation. For example, large receivable exposures require a lot more work, and may necessitate increased lender fees.

Step 4: Credit and Collection Policies

Auditors will examine a borrower's credit and collection policies, usually the information behind terms of sale. Terms of sale may be influenced by industry criteria, and range from cash before delivery to extended seasonal dating.

- *Credit approval policies:* overly conservative credit approval policies are less risky but result in fewer receivables.
- *Collection policies:* businesslike collection policies bring in cash and preserve customer goodwill.

Step 5: Analysis of Delinquencies

Lenders may substitute new receivables for those no longer acceptable as collateral. Sizable delinquent receivables deleted from a borrowing base could easily leave a borrower with the prospect of operating without customers and without lender funding.

Step 6: Evaluation of Sales

More than a few lenders and commercial finance companies fail to appreciate the value of sales analysis, not realizing that omitting this step can lead to off-the-mark forecasting. Valuable sales information is frequently buried in invoice files. There is no single way to analyze sales data, but sales should at least be broken down into categories that include geographical distribution, sales concentration, size of package, grade, class of trade, price, method (mail, telephone, and direct selling), terms (cash or charge), and order size.

Liens establish rights to collect on receivables, provided sales are legitimate, merchandise has been ordered and delivered, sales were made without warranties, and the merchandise was not shipped on consignment or subject to offset.

Step 7: Product Analysis and Product Policies

Analysis of products and product policies focuses on product planning strategies and specific product objectives and policy. Since products have life cycles, products are identified in terms of their respective life cycle's phases. For example, the start-up phase, the first phase of a product's life cycle, generally involves large-scale promotion in order to get the product off the ground, and could cause sufficient cash drain to put the capital structure at risk. Following initial success, a firm may grow rapidly and begin to earn profits (phase two). However, relatively slight added increments to equity via retained earnings generally are not enough to finance what could turn out to be a big appetite for fresh assets needed to fund anticipated rapid growth. Default risk commonly peaks at this time. Phase three, the mature or stable growth phase, is associated with reliable operations in which price and earnings are consistent with economic growth. The downside – operational success combined with low-risk acts like a magnet, attracting fresh competitors into the industry and may trigger phase four, the decline phase. Thus, product planning is continuously reviewed and centered on changes in sales volume, types and numbers of competitors, technical opportunities, patent protection, raw materials required, production load, value added, similarity to major businesses, and finally, effect on other products.

Step 8: Inventory Audit
If the audit includes an inventory examination, auditors assess inventory value – cost, market, the lower of cost or market, inventory condition, and most importantly, inventory makeup (raw materials, work-in-progress, and finished goods). Successful firms pursue an optimal inventory mix in line with order bookings, backlogs, and sales expectations. Large, out-of-balance raw material inventory points to stockpiling. Outsized work-in-process inventory usually means production problems. Worse still, partially manufactured merchandise cannot be shipped to customers. Auditors will count order backlogs against work-in-process inventory. Take heed: if order backlogs jump, customers waiting for past-due deliveries may go elsewhere.

Finally, a few words on finished goods – inventory buildup here points to product demand issues, a story in itself. Finished goods sitting on the shelf are likely inventory nobody wants. Borrowers have been known to liberalize credit standards in an effort to get the stale inventory out. Nonetheless, substituting one unproductive asset for another accomplishes little and may well lower the lien's value and reduce a borrowing base facility.

Step 9: Fixed Assets Check
This phase of the examination includes evaluation of fixed assets and the depreciation methods in use.

Step 10: Analysis of Accounts Payable and Purchases
Absence of diversity is about as risky as receivable concentrations. Slow payables are a drag on supply sources, which could be cut off at any time. Goods are not produced without supplier support; accordingly,

auditors segregate large payables, checking the payables' concentration ratios (sizable payables as a percent of total payables while measuring payables with respect to creditor, dates, amount, maturity, unusual payables, and payables agings versus receivables agings).

Step 11: Subordination Agreements

Subordination agreements are formal documents acknowledging that one party's claim or interest is inferior (junior) to that of the other party or parties. For example, a firm may agree to allow bank loans to take precedence over directors' or owners' loans to a business. Creditors review subordination agreements often because these agreements boost working capital and improve the capital structure.

Step 12: Analysis of Deposits in Cash Account

Analysis of the cash account can spot unauthorized sales of encumbered assets, withdrawal of funds for personal use, or fraudulent practices, such as unauthorized multiple assignments of receivables. Cash position determines if remittances have been diverted. Differences in unreported credits are recorded and explained.

Step 13: Lender Statement Audit

This section helps to remind us that there are few shortcuts to good auditing procedures:

- Confirm collections have been earmarked to reduce loan balances.
- Review lender statements and checks for large items, particularly those paying for travel, entertainment, vacations, and unreasonably high salaries.
- Search out large facility drawdowns that diverted funds away from the core business, such as advances to unconsolidated investments or advances to officers. Borrowing in order to boost extraneous, risky investment strategies could easily create an untenable cash position at some future date and drive the company out of business. It is, therefore, reasonable to deduce that prudent lending officers and auditors will question large withdrawals evidenced by large item checks.
- Review Federal withholding and Social Security taxes. Paid checks are cited to confirm that remittance to governmental agencies were made. Nonpayment of these obligations jeopardizes collateral positions.
- Inspect paid checks to confirm subordinated indebtedness remains intact.

Step 14: Analysis of Loans, Collateral, and Statistics

Secured lenders review facility exposures, loan balances, collateral position, and other statistics reported as part of the loan audit on at least a monthly basis. These data help to gauge the firm's peak requirements and cash needs.

Step 15: Check for Prebilling

Prebilling denotes the assignment of invoices before goods are shipped. Invoices should not be forwarded to lenders before shipment; submitting invoices to secured lenders prior to shipment date is frowned upon and comes across as a bright red flag. Lenders can easily spot prebilling by comparing shipment dates to assigned invoice dates.

Step 16: Check for Fraud

The nature of accounts receivable financing provides opportunities for dubious practices and a variety of fraud possibilities, such as assignment of fictitious accounts, accompanied by forged shipping documents; duplicate assignment of the same account; diversion of collections for the client's use; failure to report charge backs (returns and allowances); submission of false financial information; and forged shipping documents.

Step 17: Record Comparisons and Ledgering Accounts

Auditors check the borrower's records with those of the lender or lenders. Ledger accounts may reveal credit allowances and/or contra items, such as bills receivable discounted. Major discrepancies are duly noted, explained, and corrected. In ledgering accounts, auditors obtain duplicate copies of invoices together with shipping documents and/or delivery receipts. Upon receipt of satisfactory information, lenders advance the agreed percentage against receivables.

FACTORING RECEIVABLES

Factoring is an agreement between factors and suppliers of accounts receivable (retailers, wholesalers, new businesses, and manufacturers) whereby factors purchase accounts receivable and, in nonrecourse arrangements, assume responsibility for the supplier's customers' financial inability to pay. The key benefit of factoring is that it provides a quick boost to your cash flow. Instead of waiting 1–2 months for a customer payment, you now have cash to operate and grow your business. Factoring is not a loan. No debt is assumed by factoring. The financing does not show up on your balance sheet as debt and is based on the quality of your customers' credit, not your own credit or business history. Also, keep in mind that factoring provides a line of credit based on sales, not your company's net worth.

The funds are unrestricted, providing a company more flexibility than with a traditional bank loan. As needed, the factor may also provide cash advances against open receivables prior to collection. Advances generally range from 80% to 95%, depending on the industry, your credit history, and a few other benchmarks. The factor also provides back office support. Once it collects from your customers, the factor pays you the reserve balances of the invoices, minus a fee for assuming the collection risk. Factoring can be customized and managed so that it provides necessary capital when your company needs it. Unlike a conventional loan, factoring has no limit to the amount of financing. Here is a typical factoring procedure:

1. Manufacturer sells product to customers and issues invoices.
2. Invoices for which manufacturer wants immediate cash are sent to factor.
3. Factor verifies invoices with manufacturer's customers.
4. Within a day, factor advances 70–90% of the value of invoices.
5. In due course, manufacturer's customer remits payment directly to factor.
6. As the factor collects, they return the remaining 10–30% to the manufacturer less nominal servicing fees.
7. The manufacturer sells additional invoices and continues the cash flow generation cycle.

Moz Video Production is a mid-sized business specializing in corporate video and still photography. The firm needs new equipment. Unable to obtain a loan on favorable terms, management decides to sell accounts receivable to a factor on nonrecourse, notification basis. The face value of accounts receivable totals $200,000, an amount expected to convert to cash over the next 6 months. The factor determines probabilities of nonpayment and agreed to purchase receivables on a nonrecourse basis for $150,000. Moz Video pays cash for the equipment, and simultaneously reduces balance sheet risk. Remittances from customers whose accounts were sold are sent directly to the factor.

ABC Manufacturers sold $2 million accounts receivable to a factor on a notification and nonrecourse basis. Available liquidity reduced the bank credit line by $1.5 million, while the remaining $500,000 settled a portion of past-due supplier payables. Going forward, the company plans to sell new receivables, produce liquidity to finance growth, and offset factoring costs by taking advantage of supplier discounts. The bank credit line will be drawn down only in the event that the firm books unusually large orders. Working with the factor, key performance indicators improved, and as a result the firm's bank increased the credit line.

PURCHASE ORDER FINANCING

Purchase order financing is a short-term commercial finance option that provides capital to pay suppliers upfront for verified purchase orders. It lets firms – manufacturers, distributors, wholesalers, importers and exporters – accept abnormally large orders. If orders reduce, businesses can simply stop this type of financing. Purchase order financing is best used by expanding businesses with limited access to working capital that need to fulfill large orders. Here is an example of purchase order financing.

Your firm receives a large purchase order from a customer. Your supplier requires upfront payment, but the customer invoice will not be paid for another 3 months, thus straining working capital. You try to fill the working capital gap by applying for traditional financing, but cannot satisfy the bank's unsecured loan requirements. Without funding, you now risk losing both order and customer. However, now in possession of a confirmed purchase order, purchase order financing can support this single large transaction and will pay your supplier directly through a letter of credit or cash. Your business can fulfill the order, with proceeds distributed after shipment is received.

A purchase order financing company considers business history, the creditworthiness of the buyer, the ability of a supplier to produce goods, and whether or not the transaction is profitable for all parties. Although a company may be young or a start-up, management must have a proven track record of producing goods. The purchase order must be verifiable and suppliers must be familiar with the product, be able to produce it in time to meet the buyer's terms, and finally, the transaction must make a profit for all parties.

ADVANCES SECURED BY INVENTORIES

Inventory loans are secured short-term loans to purchase inventory. The three basic forms are a blanket inventory lien, a trust receipt, and field warehousing financing. A business places its inventory as collateral in exchange for an operating loan. Inventory financing is advantageous for businesses with a large amount of physical inventory ready to ship. Inventory financing is used as a stop-gap against temporary cash flow problems resulting from inventory ready to sell but not sold. It is not recommended as a long-term financing tool.

Blanket Lien on Inventory

Under a floating lien arrangement, the borrower gives the lender a lien against inventories, which is the simplest but least secure form of inventory collateral. The borrowing firm maintains full inventory, and continues to sell and replace inventory in the course of business. The lender's lack of control over inventory can dilute value as far as the lender is concerned. If a borrower is considered a poor or questionable risk, lenders may raise the ante by insisting on a blanket lien against inventory – assuming suppliers have filed no prior liens and will continue to ship behind the lender's lien. Although blanket liens provide security against all inventories, borrowers are free to dispose of inventory as long as funds are earmarked to reduce loans. Inventory-securing loans should be marketable. Marketability means that pledged inventory can sell at prices at least equal to book value or replacement cost. Most auto tires, hardware goods, and footwear are marketable, as opposed to high-tech items, where a real chance of obsolescence exists. Marketability is associated with the inventory's physical properties, as well. A warehouse full of frozen turkeys may be marketable, but the cost of storing and selling the turkeys may be prohibitive.

Price stability is another important characteristic of suitable inventory collateral. Standardized and staple durables are desirable as collateral, since these ticket items have stable prices, ready markets, and no undesirable physical properties. Perishable items create problems for sellers and lenders for obvious reasons, as do specialized items. Specialized inventories – for example, special purpose machinery, fresh produce, and advertising materials – are problematic if markets are thin. Large high-ticket items may not be desirable collateral if the expenses associated with storage and transportation are high. Commodities and products such as grain, cotton, wool, coffee, sugar, logs, lumber, canned foods, baled wood pulp, automobiles, and major appliances are acceptable collateral, whereas refrigerators-in-process are usually worthless.

Trust Receipts

A trust receipt is an instrument acknowledging that the borrower holds goods in trust for the lender. The lien is valid as long as the merchandise is in the borrower's possession and properly identified. When lenders advance funds, borrowers convey a trust receipt for the goods financed. Goods can be stored in a public warehouse or held on the premises. The borrower receives merchandise, with the lender advancing anywhere from 80% to 100% of the cost. The lender files a lien on the items financed. Documents include a list of each item along with its description and serial number. The borrower is free to sell the secured inventory but is "trusted" to remit to the lender immediately earmarked funds, which are used to repay advances plus accrued interest. In return, the lender releases the lien. The lender conducts periodic checks to ensure that the required collateral is still "in the yard." Inventory financing under trust receipts for retail sale is commonly called floor planning. For example, an automobile dealer may have arranged to finance the purchase of new cars with trust receipts.

Field Warehousing Financing

Under a field warehouse financing agreement, inventories used as collateral are physically separated from the firm's other inventories and are placed under control of a third-party field-warehousing firm. A field warehouse may take the form of a fence around a stock of raw materials, a roped-off section of the borrower's warehouse, or a warehouse constructed by the warehousing company on the borrower's premises. A terminal warehouse is located within the borrower's geographical area. It is a central warehouse used to store the merchandise of various customers. The lender generally uses a terminal warehouse when secured inventory is easily and cheaply transported to the warehouse.

A warehouse receipt allows the lender to obtain control over pledged collateral, providing the ultimate degree of security. The costs of these loans are high due to the high cost of hiring third parties (warehouse firms) to maintain and guard inventory collateral. In addition to the interest charge, the borrower must absorb the costs of warehousing by paying the warehouse fee, which is generally between 1% and 3% of the loan. When goods arrive at the warehouse designated by the lender, the warehouse official checks in the merchandise, listing each item on a warehouse receipt. Noted on the check-in list are the quantity, the serial or lot numbers, and the estimated value of the merchandise. After officials check in merchandise, the receipt is forwarded to the lender, who advances a specified percentage of the collateral value to the borrower and files a lien on all the items listed on the receipt.

The warehousing company, as the lender's agent, is responsible for seeing that the collateral pledged is actually in the warehouse. There have been occasions when warehousing companies have fraudulently issued receipts against nonexistent collateral. If this happens, and the borrower defaults, the lender ends up as an unsecured creditor. Once inventory is isolated, it is registered and the warehouse receipt is forwarded to the lender. The lender advances a specified percentage of collateral value and files a lien on the pledged security.

Regardless of whether a terminal or field warehouse is established, the warehousing company employs a security official to guard inventory. The guard or warehouse official is not permitted to release collateral without prior authorization, since lenders have total control over inventory. Only on the written approval of the lender can any portion of the secured inventory be released. Although most warehouse receipts are nonnegotiable, some are negotiable, meaning that the lender may transfer them to other parties. If the lender wants to remove a warehouse receipt loan from its books, it can sell a negotiable warehouse receipt to another party, who then replaces the original lender in the agreement. In some instances, the ability to transfer a warehouse receipt to another party may be desirable. Negotiable warehouse receipts are used to finance active inventories such as corn, cotton, and wheat. The major disadvantage of negotiable warehouse receipts is that they are easily transferred, are usually in large denominations, and must be presented to the warehouse operator each time a withdrawal is made. Therefore, lenders prefer the use of nonnegotiable receipts issued in the name of the lender for the simple reason that they provide better control of the pledged inventory.

Example of a Field Warehouse Loan Transaction

A canner of exotic fruits determines that the firm's major requirements for lender financing are during the canning season. To get the required seed capital to purchase and process an initial harvest of fruit, the canner can finance approximately 20% of its operations during the season. As cans are put into boxes and placed in storerooms, the canner realizes that additional funds are needed for labor and raw material to make the cans. Without these funds, operations will come to a grinding halt. A seasonal pattern clearly forms here. At the beginning of the fruit harvest and canning season, cash needs and loan requirements increase and reach a maximum at the termination of the canning season. Because of the canner's modest worth and substantial seasonal financing needs, the firm's lender insists on acceptable security for the funds needed to meet those needs. The services of a field warehouse company are obtained, and a field warehouse is set up.

The field warehouse company notifies the lender that the boxes of canned fruit have been shipped and checked in. At this point, the lender is assured of control over the canned goods on which loans are based and can establish a line of credit from which the canner can draw funds. As the canner receives purchase orders, it sends them to the lender. The lender then authorizes the warehouse custodian to release the boxes of canned fruit associated with the purchase orders. When the high point of the season is over, the line of credit diminishes as checks from the canner's distributors are received by the canner. This stage results in a borrowing low point, putting the canner in the low-debt position necessary before a new seasonal buildup occurs.

In certain instances, lenders may permit outstanding seasonal loans to the canner to reach an amount many times the amount of the canner's own equity capital. The fruit growers, the canner, the canner's distributors, the field warehouse company, and the lender all join forces in working out a successful distributive process to everyone's advantage. If the runoff of cash is not enough to retire seasonal loans and the canner's financial structure is sound, the lender will likely carry over the loan or loans until next season. This carryover should give the canner enough time to clean up the debt. The primary consideration for this arrangement is the fact that canned fruit is easily salable.

CHAPTER 9

What Is Your Business Worth?

Note: This chapter is available on the companion website: http://booksite. elsevier.com/9780128016985.

ABSTRACT

What is your business worth? Whether you are seeking financing, selling, acquiring, or investing in a business, your company's valuation is the number one factor. Whether you are applying for a bank loan, partnership buyout, or any other business activity, you should know how much your business is worth even if you are not planning on selling it today. If you cannot sell your business, all you have is a high-paying job. You could take for granted that you will sell your business when you retire, but if you cannot, your business does not have much value. You will have to save money for retirement in some other way. Buyers try to determine how badly you need to sell and factors in the industry and economic environment in figuring their offering price. Those extemporaneous concerns often impact the price of a small business more than they should, and not to your advantage. If you want to receive the highest price or achieve precision in valuation, get the facts, stick to the facts, and apply the valuation methods most suitable to your business.

OUTLINE

Navigating the Business Loan. http://dx.doi.org/10.1016/B978-0-12-801698-5.00008-X

ENTERPRISE'S VALUE DRIVERS

    Operating Revenue: Percent Growth

        New Products

        Health Factors/Population Demographics Associated with the Revenue Value Driver

    Cost of Sales Percent Revenues

    Net Fixed Assets

    Cost of Equity Capital

        Estimating Cost of Equity (k)

CHOOSING THE LENGTH OF THE FORECAST HORIZON

CONTINUING VALUE

TRIANGULATING RESULTS: MULTIPLES AND ALTERNATIVE VALUATION METHODS

Printed in the United States
By Bookmasters